Early Church Records

of

Dauphin County, Pennsylvania

F. Edward Wright

HERITAGE BOOKS

2018

HERITAGE BOOKS

AN IMPRINT OF HERITAGE BOOKS, INC.

Books, CDs, and more—Worldwide

For our listing of thousands of titles see our website
at
www.HeritageBooks.com

Published 2018 by
HERITAGE BOOKS, INC.
Publishing Division
5810 Ruatan Street
Berwyn Heights, Md. 20740

International Standard Book Number
Paperbound: 978-1-58549-310-4

CONTENTS

INTRODUCTION

Most of the information in this Introduction was taken from *Pastors and People* by Charles H. Glatfelter.[1] Some additional data was taken from Egle.[2]

Dauphin County was erected in 1785, from the northern townships of Lancaster County. Most of the early settlers were Scotch-Irish, and established Presbyterian Churches in Derry, Paxtang, and Hanover. The first German Church was Hill Lutheran. established in Derry Township in the mid 1750s; it was to be the only German church in the county for almost a decade.

Researchers may also be interested in the following sources:

The Chronicles of Middletown (PA). By C. H. Hutchinson. (1906).
    Repr.: Middletown Area Historical Society, P. O. Box 248,
    Middletown, PA, 17057. (Reviewed in *Our Name's The Game*
    15 (8) 2).

"Dauphin Cemetery, Dauphin, Dauphin County," by William Bell
    Clark, from Pennsylvania Genealogical Magazine 9:176-182;
    Repr. in Pennsylvania Vital Records 3:253-259

Abbreviations used in the Introduction;
ERHS: Evangelical and Reformed Historical Society, Philip Schaff
        Library, Lancaster Theological Seminary, Lancaster, PA.
LTSG: Lutheran Theological Seminary at Gettysburg.
RCR: Reformed Church Records.

THE CHURCHES

Lutheran and Reformed

FETTERHOFF'S
Halifax Township

The Lutheran and Reformed Union Congregation was started about 1788, the year the union register was begun. The first church may have been standing in 1794; it was replaced in 1858-59.

Lutheran Pastors: Michael Enderlein.
Reformed Pastors: unknown, but Glatfelter states it was almost
certainly *not* Michael Schlatter.

The Lutheran Congregation is St. Peter's, located three miles
northeast of Halifax. The Reformed Congregation joined with two
others to form The Valleys United Church of Christ, Halifax

Sources: Transcripts of registers at ERHS and LTSG.

HARRISBURG

A union congregation and school was organized in 1787. The church
was the first one in Harrisburg. The union register was begun in
1787, but after 1795 each congregation kept its own registers. In
1816 the Reformed Congregation purchased the Lutheran share of
the church. Egle, p. 329, gives a list of the first subscribers.

Lutheran Pastors: Frederick Schaefer, 1787-1790; Peter Bentz, 1792-
1794.
Reformed Pastors: Anthony Hautz, 1790-1797.

The Lutheran Congregation is Zion Lutheran Church. The Reformed
Church is now the Salem United Church of Christ.

Sources: RCR 11 at EHRS; Theodore Emanuel Schmauk. *A History
of the Lutheran Church in Pennsylvania (1638-1820)...*
Philadelphia. 1903.

HILL, MAXE
Derry Township

The Lutheran Congregation was the first German congregation in
Dauphin County and was established in the mid 1750's. The first
church was built in 1767, and the register was started in 1757 by
Theophilus Engelland. It includes some pastoral acts performed

earlier.

Pastors included: Theophilus Engelland, c.1757-1768; Daniel Kuhn, 1769; Michael Enderlein, 1770-1776; Casper Stoever, 1776-1779; Frederick Melsheimer, 1779-1783; and Casper Hoerner, 1787-1794.

The congregation is now known as St. Paul's Church, about two miles out of Hummelstown.

Sources: *Records of the "Hill" Lutheran Church...* . Ed. by E. W. S. Parthemore. Harrisburg: 1892. *Saint Paul's Evangelical Lutheran Church Register...Parish Registers, 1757-1866.* 1976. David S. Martin. *History of St. Paul's (Sand Hill) Lutheran Church...* . 1952.

HOFFMAN'S LYKENS VALLEY
Lykens Township

The Reformed Congregation was established in the 1780s. A paper taken from the cornerstone c.1885-87, says that the church was "founded, 1771," but there is no other proof of this date. The register was begun in 1791, but contains some earlier baptisms. Irish gives Marriages for the Hoffman Reformed Church, Lykens Valley, 1781-1855.

Pastors included: Samuel Dubendorff and Anthony Hautz.

The congregation is now called St. Peter's United Church of Christ, two miles east of Berrysburg.

Sources: RCR 11 at EHRS. *200th Anniversary (1771-1971). St. Peter's United Church of Christ (Hoffman's Church)...* . 1971.

HUMMELSTOWN
Derry Township

In 1766 the German Evangelical Lutheran Congregation purchased two lots in Frederick Town for a church, school, and burial ground.

In 1766 the German Reformed Presbyterian Congregation also purchased a lot of land in Frederick Town.

The Lutheran register was begun in 1766, but some earlier baptisms were also included. The earliest surviving Reformed register begins in 1808.

Lutheran Pastors were: Theophilus Engelland, c.1766-1768, Casper Stoever, 1768-c.1770; Michael Enderlein, 1770-1779; and William Kurtz, 1781-1795.
Reformed Pastors were: Conrad Bucher, 1765-1768; and William Runkel, 1777-1781.

The Lutheran Congregation, at West and North Rosanna Sts., is Zion. The Reformed Congregation is Hummelstown United Church of Christ.

Source: Translation of register, LTSG.

KLINGER'S
Lykens Township

The union congregation can be traced to 1787, when a union register was begun. An agreement between the two denominations dated 1801 contains a sketch showing a church and graveyard. The union church was dissolved in 1968.

The Lutheran congregation is Zion, one mile south of Klinger's.

Source: Translation of register, LTSG.

LYKENS VALLEY
Upper Paxton Township

The congregations date from the mid 1770s. In March 1775 Adam King and George Nagles were granted a warrant for 160 acres in trust for the first Presbyterian and Lutheran churches "where their Houses are already built."

The Lutheran register include baptisms from 1770.

The Reformed register was started in 1774.

The Lutheran Pastors included: Michael Enderlein, c.1770-c.1793; and John Grobp, 1794.
The Reformed Pastors included: William Hendel, 1774-1779; Samuel Dubendorff, 1779-1782; and Anthony Hautz, 1796.

The Lutheran congregation is Salem. The Reformed Congregation is David's. Both are located northeast of Millersburg on Route 25.

Sources: RCR 11 EHRS; pamphlet on 200th anniversary of the
     Lutheran Congregation; pamphlet on the 180th anniversary
     of the Reformed Congregation.

LYKENS VALLEY, ST. JOHN'S
(Orig.) Upper Paxton, (now) Mifflin Township

The Lutheran congregation was begun in 1780. The register was started by Michael Enderlein in 1791. The church was built between 1797 and 1800. The Lutheran Pastors included: Michael Enderlein, 1780-1807 (Egle, p. 454).

Source: Translation of register, LTSG.

MIDDLETOWN
Lower Swatara Township

In September 1764 the land on which the church was to be built (Lot 135 in Middletown) was deeded to three men, and a few weeks later Governor John Penn gave two others a license to collect money to defray the cost of the building of a place of worship to be called St. Peters. Work on the church began in 1767.

A register was started in 1794. Earlier records can be found in the Hummelstown Register and in the Private Register of Traugott Illing.

The Lutheran Pastors included: Theophilus Engelland, 1764-1768; Casper Stoever, 1768-1770; Daniel Kuhn, 1770; Traugott illing, 1773-

1788; William Kurtz, 1788-1792; and Peter Bentz, 1792-1795. The Lutheran congregation is St. Peter's, Middletown.

Sources: *Register of Marriages and Baptisms Kept by the Rev. Traugott Frederick Illing*. Harrisburg: 1891. Translation of Hummelstown register, LTSG. Pamphlet on 200th Anniversary.

PAXTON
Lower Paxton Township

The congregations were organized in the early 1780s. In 1797 one acre, fifty perches of land was sold to the "trustees of the United German Lutheran and Reformed Church in the Township of Paxton. The union arrangement lasted until c.1924-26.

The Lutheran Pastors included: Frederick Melsheimer, 1783-1785 and Frederick Schaefer, 1786-1790.
The Reformed Pastors included: Anthony Hautz, 1791-1797.

The Lutheran congregation is St. Mark's, 4200 Londonderry.
The Reformed Congregation is Colonial Park United Church of Christ, 5000 Devonshire Road, Harrisburg.

Sources: William Henry Egle. *Notes and Queries... . Third Series,* 1:179-184, 186-191, 194-199, 202-207.

WENRICH'S
Lower Paxton Township

The congregations were organized about 1791, according to a register which started that year. In 1793 land was deeded for the United Congregations of High Church (i.e., Lutheran) and Presbyterians to build a church, school and a graveyard.

Lutheran Pastors include: William Kurtz, c1791-c1794.
Reformed Pastors include; Anthony Hautz, 1791-1797.

The Lutheran Congregation is Christ Lutheran Church.
The Reformed Congregation is now known as St. Thomas United
Church of Christ.

Sources: "With the Forefathers of Wenrich's Church... " (1922); *The
History of St. Thomas UCC. Formerly Wenrich's Evangelical
and Reformed Church... . 1957*

Presbyterian

CONEWAGO CHURCH
near Gainesburg

The church was erected c.1741 (Egle, p. 420). Early pastors: Samuel
Black, 1741-

DERRY CHURCH

This congregation was established c.1729, Paxtang was set off from it
c.1738 (Egle, p. 413). Early pastors were: William Bertram, 1738-
1742; John Elder, 1748-1792; Nathaniel R. Snowden, 1793-1795;
Joshua Williams, 1798.

HANOVER CHURCH
Conewago Township

The church was established in the 1730s. A register was kept by Rev.
Snodgrass (Egle, pp. 430-31).

Early pastors: Richard Sankey, 1738-1759; John Steel and John
Elder, 1759; Robert McMordie, 1762-c.1765; William Thom, 1772;
Matthew Woods, 1781-1784; James Snodgrass, 1787-.

MARKET SQUARE CHURCH
Harrisburg

The church was established by the Presbytery of Carlisle in 1787 (Egle, p. 336). Early pastors included: John Elder, 1787-1792; Nathaniel R. Snowden, 1794-.

PAXTANG CHURCH

A Church was standing as early as 1732 when the Presbytery of Donegal was established (Egle, p. 394). For a discussion of the differences between Old Side and New Side Presbyterians, see Egle, pp. 395-396.

Early pastors included: William Bertram, 1732-1738; Mr. Sankey, Mr. Alexander, Mr. Craven, and Mr. Elder, 1738; John Elder, 1738-

Robert W. Barnes

NOTES

1. Except where otherwise noted, material for this Introduction was based on *Pastors and People, Volume I: Pastors and Congregations.* By Charles H. Glatfelter. Breinigsville: The Pennsylvania German Society, 1980.

2. *History Of The Counties Of Dauphin And Lebanon In The Commonwealth Of Pennsylvania: Biographical And Genealogical.* By William Henry Egle, M.D., M.A. Philadelphia: Everts & Peck, 1883. Cited as Egle.

MAP OF DAUPHIN COUNTY

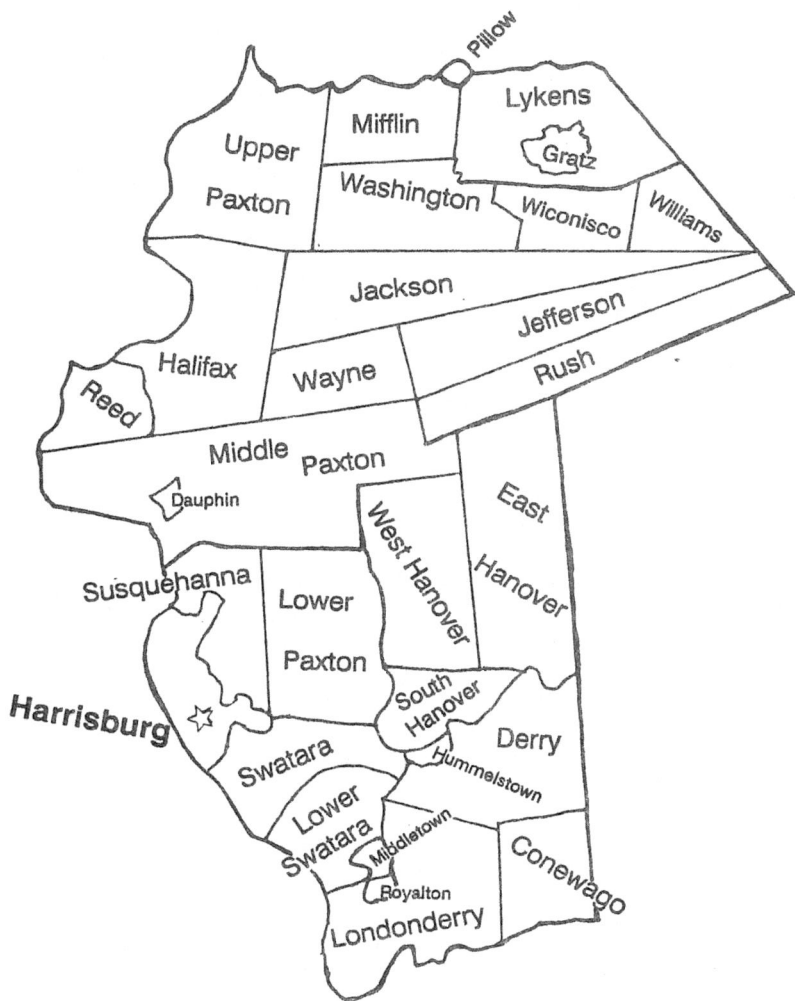

Pillow

Lykens

Upper

Mifflin

Gratz

Paxton

Washington

Wiconisco

Williams

Jackson

Jefferson

Halifax

Wayne

Rush

Reed

Middle Paxton

Dauphin

East

Hanover

Susquehanna

Lower

West Hanover

Paxton

Harrisburg

South
Hanover

Derry

Swatara

Hummelstown

Lower
Swatara

Middletown

Conewago

Royalton

Londonderry

SALEM REFORMED CHURCH, HARRISBURG

Baptisms by Rev. Anthony Hautz, 1790-1797

Susanna of Christian Gunckel and Anna Catharine, b. May 31, 1790. Spon: Anna Catharine Heyer.

Catherine of Gottlieb Gottschall and Sabina, b. May 8, 1790. Spon: parents.

John Philip of Andrew Schwalm and Susanna, b. Mar 24, 1790. Spon: parents.

Elizabeth of Jacob Ernst and Susanna Philippina, b. Feb 10, 1790. Spon: George Hartman and Elizabeth.

Catherine of Martin Lengel and Elizabeth, b. Jun 25, 1790; bapt. Jul 4, 1790. Spon: Martin Koppenhafer and Susanna.

John of John Christian Gunckel and Anna Catherine, b. Apr 29, 1788. Spon: John Comfort(?).

Anna Maria and Rebecca, twins, of Henry Bohl and Margaret, b. Apr 24, 1788. Spon: John George Leru and John Bohl and Elizabeth.

Elizabeth of Matthew Neidig and Catherine, b. Apr 10, 1788. Spon: parents.

Susanna of Henry Brunner and Susanna, b. May 4, 1788. Spon: parents.

John of Leonard Schwartz and Elizabeth, b. Aug 31, 1788. Spon: Casper Schwartz.

Maria Barbara of George Lischer and Anna, b. Jan 23, 1788. Spon: Maria Leru.

Anna Maria of George Schuedter and Catharine, b. Aug 30, 1788. Spon: John Woermly and Maria.

Michael of John Ebert and Elizabeth, b. Sep 10, 1788. Spon: George Haier and Catherine.

Anna Sabina of John Nicholas Martin and Maria Regina, b. Sep 23, 1788. Spon: Anna Maria Kissey.

John of George Schuedter and Elizabeth, b. Jan 25, 1789. Spon: Jacob Fleur and Elizabeth.

Maria Elizabeth of Henry Kissner and Veronica, b. Oct 18, 1788. Spon: Sabina Kissner.

John Peter of Wendel Breininger and Margaret, b. Oct 10, 1788. Spon: Juliana Charlotte Brunner.

Catherine Elizabeth of Jacob Dege and Barbara, b. Jan 17, 1789. Spon: Regina Martin.

Magdalene of George Schallhamer and Magdalene, b. Jan 16, 1789. Spon: Christian Schwenck and Affre.

John of John Comfoet and Philippina, b. Jul 27, 1789. Spon: George Redig and Maria.

Mary Elizabeth of John Denzel and Eva Catherine, b. Oct 26, 1788. Spon: Maria Eliz. Hahn.

Maria Margaret of Jacob Hatz and Catherine, b. Oct 11, 1789. Spon: Margaret Hatz.

Barbara of Christian Ewig and Christine, b. Apr 5, 1790; bapt. Aug 28, 1790. Spon: Barbara Ewig.

Elizabeth of Henry Rothraf and Magdalene, b. Apr 20, 1790. Spon: parents.

---- of Michael von Kennen and wife, b. 1790. Spon: George Hayer and Catherine.

John George of John Meyer and Magdalene, b. Aug 1, 1790. Spon: George Hartman and Elizabeth.

John Matthew of Englehart Woermle and Elizabeth, b. Sep 25, 1790. Spon: John Matthew Gast and Anna Margaret.

Jacob of Christian Schupp and Elizabeth, b. Jun 25, 1790. Spon: Matthew Wintnagel and Maria.

Anna Maria of John Ebert and Elizabeth, b. Apr 15, 1790. Spon: Christian Gunckel and Catherine.

Elizabeth of Peter Miller and Elizabeth, b. May 11, 1790. Spon: parents.

Elizabeth of Henry Stuentze and Anna Elizabeth, b. Sep 29, 1790. Spon: Elizabeth Bischof.

John of Conrad Schmitt and Margaret, b. Sep 29, 1790. Spon: John Albert and Maria Barbara.

Anna Maria of Michael Nertzer and Elizabeth, b. Oct 28, 1789. Spon: George Lerruh and Anna Maria.

Jacob of Jacob Flauer and Elizabeth, b. Dec 29, 1790. Spon: George Hautz and Margaret.

Anna Maria of Michael Offlinger and Barbara, b. Oct 30, 1790. Spon: Catherine Rihmer.

Lydia of John Bleimeier, b. Dec 19, 1790. Spon: Catherine Schram.

Martha of John Norten and Susan, b. Sep 24, 1789. Spon: parents.

John of Henry Kunrath and Elizabeth, b. Jan 9, 1791. Spon: John Kiblinger and Elizabeth.

Salome of George Jaus and Maria, b. Jan 16, 1791. Spon: Frederick Jaus and Salome.

--- of Michael Peter and Elizabeth, b. Dec 8, 1790. Spon: parents.

Maria of John Freysinger and Elizabeth, b. Feb 24, 1791. Spon: Henry Rothraf and Mary Magdalene.

Catherine of George Huwer and Barbara, b. Nov 17, 1788. Spon: Conrad Kissinger and Barbara.

Susanna of Conrad Kissinger and Barbara, b. Dec 10, 1790. Spon: parents.

John of Abraham Huy and Magdalene, b. Oct 26, 1790. Spon: parents.

Jacoby of Bernard Morvy and wife, b. Aug 4, 1790. Spon: Abraham Huy.

John of George Lyscher and Anna, b. Oct 23, 1790. Spon: Henry Staenz and Anna Elizabeth.

Daniel of Frederick Schweitzer and Catherine, b. Feb 21, 1791. Spon: parents.

John George of Christopher Martin Ely and Margaret, b. Nov 21, 1790. Spon: Jacob Ebrecht and Hannah.

John Augustus of Andrew Grauss and Barbara, b. Mar 19, 1970. Spon: parents.

Elizabeth of John Schissler and Margaret, b. Sep 2, 1790. Spon: Elizabeth Wermly.

John George of John Weis and Elizabeth, b. Mar 20, 1791. Spon: John Woermly and Anna Maria.

Peter of John Toerner and Magdalene, b. Oct 18, 1789. Spon: Elizabeth Trabinger.

Susanna of George Haier and Catherine, b. Nov 21, 1789. Spon: Christian Kunckel and Catherine.

Maria Eva of Henry Brunner and Susanna, b. Mar 3, 1791. Spon: parents.

Jacob of Jacob Zollinger and Rosina, b. Mar 22, 1791. Spon: parents.

Elizabeth of Philip Stenz and Catherine, b. Apr 28, 1791. Spon: Joseph Keller and Elizabeth.

John of Nicholas Stroh and Maria, b. Oct 4, 1790. Spon: parents.

Jacob of Gottlieb Spohn and Catherine, b. Jan 29, 1791. Spon: Jacob Hatz and Catherine.

Anna Barbara of Adam Hacker and Maria, b. Apr 26, 1791. Spon: George Schacky and Anna Barbara.

William of Mansfield Bandon and Elizabeth, b. May 30, 1791. Spon: Michael von Kennen.

Catherine of Jacob Roland and Catherine, b. Nov 8, 1791. Spon:

Jonas Rupp and Maria Elizabeth.

Anna Barbara of George Pannekuche and Anna, b. Jul 2, 1791. Spon: mother.

John of Peter Unger and Magdalene, b. Jul 12, 1791. Spon: John Leinbach and Maria.

Peter of Philip Riel and Catherine, b. Jul 18, 1791. Spon: Peter Walter.

George Peter of Daniel Luckes and Eva, b. May 1, 1791. Spon: parents.

Samuel of Christopher Sies and Elizabeth, b. Jul 3, 1791. Spon: Stephen Hornung and Eva.

Catherine of Daniel Krieger and Catherine, b. Jun 10, 1791. Spon: Charlotte Wallauer.

Susanna of John Heiss and Barbara, b. Aug 21, 1791. Spon: Margaret Misch.

John of John Franck and wife, b. May 27, 1789. Spon: Jacob Walter.

Henry of Peter Walborn and Catherine, b. Sep 21, 1791. Spon: Henry Conrad and Elizabeth.

Samuel of Conrad Dieter and Elizabeth, b. Oct 20, 1791. Spon: Abraham Lang and Maria.

Samuel of John George Pfrimmer and Elizabeth, b. Jun 29, 1790. Spon: Jacob Senn and Elizabeth.

Elizabeth of (Rev) A. Hautz and Catherine, b. Sep 28, 1791. Spon: Elizabeth Baecker.

Henry of John Woermly and Maria, b. Sep 5, 1791. Spon: parents.

Maria Margaret of Sebastian Wagner and Margaret, b. Jul 13, 1791. Spon: Anna Maria Eideneier.

Mary Magdelene of John Schitz and Maria, b. Jan 21, 1791. Spon: Mary Magdalene Engler and Fred. Schitz.

Isaac of Isaac Kunz and Margaret, b. Nov 23, 1791. Spon: parents.

Maria of Frederick Jaus and Salome, b. Oct 1, 1791. Spon: Jacob Jaus and Maria.

Philippina of Felix Lih (Lee?) and Margaret, b. Aug 28, 1791. Spon: parents.

Elizabeth of Matthew Huttman and Catherine, b. Jan 1, 1792. Spon: Magdalene Harter.

Michael of George Ziegler and Elizabeth, b. Jan 28, 1792. Spon: Margaret Kunz.

John of George Englert and Mary Magdalene, b. Feb 7, 1791. Spon: John Schitz and Maria.

Susanna of Henry Baeder and Margaret, b. Apr 1, 1792. Spon:
Susanna Huber.

George of John Schuesler and Margaret, b. Dec 23, 1792. Spon:
parents.

Sarah of Philip Heck and Elizabeth, b. Mar 27, 1792. Spon: Gertrude
Breis.

John of John Zulauf and Margaret, b. Jan 3, 1792. Spon: Philip Heck.

John of Adam Hart and Rosina, b. Mar 31, 1792. Spon: Conrad Lang
and Anna Rosina.

Elizabeth of Christian Lang and Maria, b. Feb 3, 1792. Spon: parents.

William of John Haas and Catherine, b. Mar 30, 1792. Spon: Michael
Zoeller and Christian Jung.

George of George Friedly and Anna, b. May 28, 1792. Spon: parents.

Rebecca of Michael Bool (Pool) and Anna, b. Mar 14, 1792. Spon:
Ludwig Degen and Juliana.

John Jacob of John Pfuhl and Mary Magdalene, b. Mar 7, 1792.
Spon: Jacob Welschhans and Maria.

John Henry of Henry Kissner and Veronica, b. Nov 6, 1791. Spon:
George Leruh and Anna Maria.

Anna Maria of Christian Kunckel and Catherine, b. Jun 19, 1792.
Spon: George Hayer and Catherine.

Charlotte of Jacob Jaus and Catherine, b. Jul 10, 1792. Spon: the
father and Catherine Jaus.

Elizabeth of John Buechler and Elizabeth, b. Apr 7, 1792. Spon:
Leonard Buechler and Elizabeth.

Salome of John Ebert and Elizabeth, b. May 3, 1792. Spon: parents.

John George of George Bucher and Elizabeth, b. Mar 24, 1792. Spon:
parents.

Gottfried (Godfrey) of Gottfried Eberhart and Catherine, b. May 9,
1792. Spon: Philip Dindorf.

William of Valentine Wengert and Margaret, b. Sep 27, 1792. Spon:
parents.

Susanna of George Heyger and Catherine, b. Nov 22, 1789. Spon:
Christian Kunckel and Catherine.

Margaret of John Schitz and Maria, b. Jul 22, 1792. Spon: John
Trally and Margaret.

John of Joseph Poth and Elizabeth, b. Mar 27, 1790. Spon: Nicholas
Schmit and Maria Margaret.

Joseph of Joseph Poth and Elizabeth, b. Apr 31, 1791. Spon: parents.

Elizabeth of Jonathan Clauer and Anna Maria, b. Jul 16, 1792. Spon:

Jacob Woelfly and Catherine.

Maria of Joseph Goseph(?) and wife, b. Jun 9, 1792. Spon: Adam Riffer and Catherine Goseph.

Anna of Peter Ober and Catherine, b. Dec 30, 1792. Spon: Anna Ober.

George of Michael Nertzer and Elizabeth, b. Oct 15, 1791. Spon: George Leru and Maria.

Jacob of Engelhart Woermly and Elizabeth, b. Nov 23, 1792. Spon: Jacob Woermly and Elizabeth.

John of Henry Seiler and Catherine, b. Aug 20, 1791. Spon: Frederick Pflicht and Christine.

George of Jacob Haenning and Magdalene, b. Dec 12, 1792. Spon: Jacob Bucher and Susanna.

Frederick of Henry Steinbring and Linn Lora, b. Dec 4, 1792. Spon: parents.

Maria of Henry Rathraf and Magdalene, b. Oct 28, 1792. Spon: parents.

John William of Philip Riel and Catherine, b. Jan 13, 1793. Spon: Peter Boob and Elizabeth.

John Conrad of Jacob Bucher and Susanna, b. Dec 28, 1792. Spon: parents.

Jacob and Sarah of George Heyger and Catherine, b. Feb 13, 1793, bapt. Feb 13, 1793. Spon: Jacob Reitzel, Henry Liebhart and Catherine.

Jacob of Nicholas Schahberg and Barbara, b. Feb 22, 1793. Spon: parents.

Lydia of George Jaus and Maria, b. Feb 28, 1793. Spon: Catherine Jaus.

Anna Margaret of George Renninger and Elizabeth, b. Feb 11, 1793. Spon: George Renninger and Catherine Benetsch.

Samuel of John Pool and Polly, b. Feb 1, 1793. Spon: Jacob Welschhans and Mary Magdalene.

Catherine of John Miésch and Magdalene, b. Feb 1, 1793. Spon: John Heiss and Barbara.

Sarah of John Hacker and Catherine, b. Dec 6, 1793. Spon: parents.

Jacob of Jacob Ebrecht and Hannah, b. Apr 10, 1792. Spon: Ludwig Schneiter and Rosina.

Henry of Christopher Sies and Elizabeth, b. Feb 2, 1793. Spon: Philip Hornung.

John Henry of Jonas Graff and Elizabeth, b. Feb 17, 1793. Spon:

Catherine Schweitzer.

John of Andrew Rihm and Maria, b. Apr 6, 1793. Spon: parents.

Elizabeth of Frederick Zerbe and Susanna, b. Feb 22, 1793. Spon: Adam Leyer and Eva Margaret.

Maria of John Fessler and Catherine, b. Apr 12, 1793. Spon: Jacob Fessler and Catherine.

John George of Frederick Huebscher and Maria, b. Mar 27, 1793. Spon: parents.

Elizabeth of John Krall and Sarah, b. Mar 13, 1793. Spon: Mother.

Henry of Henry Conrad and Elizabeth, b. May 1, 1793. Spon: Peter Walborn and Catherine.

Simon of Conrad Straser and Esther, b. Apr 14, 1793. Spon: George Scheuly and Catherine.

Maria Veronica of Henry Kissner and Froehne (Verena), b. Mar 29, 1793. Spon: Maria Elizabeth Bindnagel.

John Peter of Daniel Schneider and Anna, b. Oct 3, 1792. Spon: Henry Kissner and Veronica.

George of Daniel Schweickert and Catherine, b. Feb 6, 1793. Spon: Father.

Salome of George Armstang and Catherine, b. Jan 14, 1793. Spon: Sabina Kissner.

Andrew of Peter Daubenheier and Christine, b. Mar 13, 1792. Spon: Philip Braun and Barbara.

George David of Christopher Wolters and Christine, b. Jan 12, 1793. Spon: parents.

Elizabeth of John Zinn and Catherine, b. Apr 8, 1793. Spon: parents.

Elizabeth of Carl Burneisen and Catherine, b. Aug 21, 1792. Spon: Jacob Clauer and Elizabeth.

Maria of Jacob Friedly and Elizabeth, b. Oct 5, 1790. Spon: John Kraus and Catherine.

Samuel of Jacob Friedly and Elizabeth, b. Aug 24, 1792. Spon: ----.

Anna Maria of Jacob Eigelberger and Anna Maria, b. Apr 1, 1793. Spon: Anna Maria Ruppli.

John George of George Loescher and Anna, b. Oct 20, 1792. Spon: George Leruh and the mother.

John of John Brenner and Magdalene, b. Aug 12, 1793. Spon: parents.

Anna Maria of John Ritz and Catherine, b. Jul 8, 1793. Spon: parents.

John of Stephen Horn and Eva, b. Jul 13, 1793. Spon: Catherine

Basler.

John Adam of John Schupp and Elizabeth, b. Jul 29, 1793. Spon: John Adam Diefenbach.

Susanna of John Weis and Elizabeth, b. Aug 22, 1793. Spon: George Soermly and Elizabeth. [This should probably be Woermly]

Anna of George Wormely and Elizabeth, b. Sep 19, 1973. Spon: Jacob Woermly and Elizabeth.

Catherine of Henry Petry and Magdalene, b. Oct 18, 1793. Spon: parents.

John of John Heist and Barbara, b. Sep 10, 1793. Spon: John Miesch and Magdalene.

Simon of Frederick Rupply and Margaret, b. Jun 18, 1793. Spon: Simon Schneider and Margaret Rupple.

Joseph of John Geo. Diefenbach and Elizabeth, b. Oct 8, 1793. Spon: Joseph Keller and Elizabeth.

Catherine of George Peffer and Susanna Maria, b. Oct 15, 1793. Spon: Susanna Huber.

John George of Daniel Lucas and Eva, b. Nov 9, 1793. Spon: George Fackler and Susanna.

Eva of Martinus Spengler and Christine, b. Jan 19, 1794. Spon: William Faber and Christine.

Jacob of John Norten and Susanna, b. Sep 17, 1793. Spon: parents.

William of Nicholas Staug and Margaret, b. Nov 14, 1793. Spon: William Schaeffer.

Elizabeth of George Bucher and Elizabeth, b. Jan 22, 1794. Spon: parents.

John Jacob of Henry Stentz and Elizabeth, b. Jan 26, 1794. Spon: Ludwig Degen and Jul. Charlotte.

Ephraim of Jacob Bayer and Anna, b. Jul 24, 1793. Spon: John Holtz and Barbara.

George of Frederick Schupp and Elizabeth, b. Jan 16, 1794. Spon: George Ness.

Sarah of John Denzel and Eva Catherine, b. Nov 22, 1794(?). Spon: parents.

George of Adam Hacker and Anna Maria, b. Jan 21, 1794. Spon: parents.

Henry of John Baldly and Margaret, b. Jan 28, 1794. Spon: parents.

John Daniel of Andrew Greus and Barbara, b. Feb 2, 1794. Spon: Mother.

Catherine of George Weibel and Anna Maria, b. Mar 25, 1794. Spon:

parents.

John of Frederick Kistler and Elena, b. Sep 18, 1792. Spon: Jacob Stricker.

Anna of Frederick Kistler and Elena, b. Jan 2, 1794. Spon: Elizabeth Dindorf.

George of John Fackler and Elizabeth, b. Apr 25, 1794. Spon: George Fackler.

Conrad of Michael Rupply and Elizabeth, b. Aug 18, 1793. Spon: Mother.

Adam of Joseph Poth and Elizabeth, b. ---, 1793. Spon: Maria Margaret Schmitt.

John Henry of John Puhl and Maria, b. May 10, 1794. Spon: Jacob Puhl and Anna Maria.

Catherine of George Cassel and Sabina, b. Feb 21, 1794. Spon: parents.

David of Isaac Kuntz and Margaret, b. Aug 16, 1793. Spon: parents.

John of Samuel Gorlitz and Anna Maria Magdalena, b. Dec 2, 1793. Spon: parents.

George of Jacob Flauers and Elizabeth, b. May 1, 1794. Spon: Peter Bayer and Margaret.

Margaret of Jacob Staug and Catherine, b. Aug 19, 1974. Spon: Nicholas Staug and Margaret.

Adam of Joseph Poth and Elizabeth, b. Oct 12, 1793. Spon: Margaret Schmitt.

Elizabeth of John Schitz and Maria, b. Sep 13, 1794. Spon: Joseph Poth and Elizabeth.

George of Christopher Sies and Elizabeth, b. Dec 25 1794. Spon: George Ziegler and Elizabeth.

Maria of George Ziegler and Elizabeth, b. Dec 5, 1794. Spon: Christopher Sies and Elizabeth.

John Philip of Jacob Reitzel and Barbara, b. Dec 19, 1794. Spon: John Reitzel.

Peter of John Beck and Barbara, b. Sep 26, 1794. Spon: parents.

John of Lorentz Benetsh and Anna, b. Feb 18, 1794. Spon: Henry Liphart and wife.

Frederick of John Weiser and Justina, b.Sep 24, 1794. Spon: Jacob Ebrecht and Hannah.

Elizabeth of John Zollinger and Catherine, b. Feb 15, 1796. Spon: parents.

Maria Sarah of John Zinn and Catherine, b. Jan 31, 1795. Spon:

Henry Brunner and Susanna.

Elizabeth of Henry Brunner and Susanna, b. Sep 19, 1793. Spon: parents.

Elizabeth of John Zinn and Catherine, b. Apr 8, 1793. Spon: parents.

Maria Elizabeth of Jacob Bucher and Susanna, b. Apr 23, 1795. Spon: parents.

Anna of George Seydel and Elizabeth, b. Apr 29, 1794. Spon: Jacob Ebrecht and Hannah.

Samuel of John Kapp and Sarah, b. Jan 4, 1796. Spon: parents.

Magdalene of Leonard Wallauer and Susanna, b. Nov 26, 1794. Spon: parents.

Sibylla of George Reitzel and Maria, b. May 24, 1796. Spon: Barbara Libisin (Libi).

Anna Maria of Henry Liphart and Catherine, b. Jun 30, 1796. Spon: Jacob Schultz and Anna Maria.

Henry of Henry Liphart and Catherine, b. May 26, 1793. Spon: parents.

Maria Elizabeth of Frederick Windnagel and Eva, b. Feb 1, 1796. Spon: The father and Elizabeth Windnagel.

John Jacob of Henry Brunner and Susanna, b. Apr 16, 1796. Spon: Margaret Bolliger.

John of John Miesch and Magdalene, b. Oct 20, 1796. Spon: John Zollinger and Catherine.

Elizabeth of Henry Baeder and Margaret, b. Jan 1, 1797. Spon: parents.

Elizabeth of John Ermold and Maria, b. Feb 25, 1797. Spon: John Gerberich.

Joseph of Martin Spengler and Christine, b. Feb 22, 1797. Spon: parents.

George of Daniel Schweickert and Catherine, b. Nov 3, 1796. Spon: parents.

Elizabeth of Peter Ermold and Magdalene, b. Apr 4, 1797. Spon: Peter Bayer and Margaret.

Elizabeth of Peter Kaub and Elizabeth, b. Dec 29, 1797. Spon: Frena (Verena) Schaefer.

Maria of John Portimor and Catherine Elizabeth, b. Apr 2, 1797. Spon: Regina Portimor.

Anna Maria of Walter Jonsly and Susanna, b. Nov 10, 1796. Spon: George Leruh and Anna Maria.

Elizabeth of Martin Renninger and Margaret, b. Dec 6, 1796. Spon:

parents.

Anna Margaret of George Mayer and Anna Maria, b. Feb 23, 1796. Spon: Margaret Schmith.

John of Henry Petry and Magdalene, b. Jan 29, 1797. Spon: Simon Schneider and Catherine.

John of John Schecksbeer and Rebecca, b. Jun 2, 1797. Spon: George Saily and Catherine.

Elizabeth of George Hatz and Catherine, b. Aug 19, 1796. Spon: parents.

Maria of Lorentz Benetsch and Anna, b. Nov 26, 1796. Spon: Tobias Saiboth and Christine.

William of John Puhl and Maria, b. Jul 7, 1797. Spon: Elizabeth Welschans.

Elizabeth of Martin Alleman and Rosina, b. Sep 5, 1797. Spon: Elizabeth Miller.

Baptisms by various persons 1797-1808

Margaret of John Zinn and Catherine, b. Jun 13, 1797. Spon: Elizabeth Gruenewalt.

Anna Catherine of Jacob Zollinger and Rosina, b. Jul 18, 1797. Spon: parents.

Adam of Henry Orth and Rebecca, b. Apr 22, 1799; bapt. Jan 21, 1800. Spon: parents.

Henry of Peter Kunckel and Eva, b. Jan 6, 1800, bapt. ---- by Rev. Mr. Hautz.

George of Peter Kunckel and Eva, b. Oct 11, 1796, bapt. 1800.

Baptisms by Rev. Philip Gloninger 1808-1815

Elizabeth of David Krause and Regina, b. Sep 20, 1792; bapt. Aug 10, 1808. Spon: Catherine Gloninger and Elizabeth Keller.

Adam of Gideon Kober and Veronica, b. May 28, 1781; bapt. Nov 16, 1808.

David of Gideon Kober and Veronica, b. Nov 12, 1783; bapt. Nov 16, 1808.

Jacob of Gideon Kober and Veronica, b. Oct 22, 1786, bapt. Nov 16, 1808.

Catherine of Gideon Kober and Veronica, b. Apr 13, 1790; bapt. Nov 16, 1808.

Penelope of Thomas Atkinson and Salome, b. Aug 10, 1787; bapt. Apr 21, 1809. Spon: Catechumen.

Susanna (wife of William Fremolle), of Thomas Atkinson and Salome, Oct 16, 1789; bapt. Apr 21, 1809. Spon: Catechumen.

MARRIAGES by Rev. Anthony Hautz 1791-1792

Sep 20, 1791, George Bucher and Elizabeth Kiblinger.

Dec 6, 1791, Jacob Graf and Elizabeth Schweitzer.

Nov 29, 1791, John Stauffer and Anna Heichert.

Jan 2, 1792, John Fogelgesang & Maria Ming.

Feb 12, 1792, Anthony Seifer and Patty Martn.

BURIALS

Samuel Hocker, b. Aug 10, 1774, d. Nov 2, 1808; bur. on Scherer's cemetery, Paxton. Left widow and 7 children.

Salome Mayer, wife of Benjamin Mayer, b. Jan 7, 1755, d. Mar 27, 1809, bur. Mar 28, 1809. Left 2 sons and 6 daus.

Maria Cath. Eglee nee Bintling, widow of --- Eglee, b. Jan 18, 1746, d. Jan 30, 1810, bur. Feb 1, 1810.

Elizabeth Doll, wife of John Doll, b. Jun 7, 1742, d. Feb 9, 1810, bur. Feb 11, 1810. Left 6 sons and 1 dau.

Christine Schiffer, wife of John Schiffer, b. Jan 13, 1750, d. Mar 9, 1810, bur. Mar 11, 1810. Left husband and 7 children.

Abraham Huey, b. Mar --, 1745, d. Apr 3, 1810, bur. Apr 5, 1810. Left wife and 9 children.

Elizabeth Huey, dau of late Abraham Huey and wife Magdalene, b. May 5, 1793, d. Apr 11, 1810, bur. Apr. 13, 1810.

Susanna Schultz, dau of Jacob Schultz and wife Anna Maria, b. Jul 4, 1797, d. Apr 21, 1810, bur. Apr 23, 1810.

Elizabeth Hock, widow, b. ca 1754, d. Apr 9, 1809, bur. Apr 10, 1809. Left 4 sons and 1 dau.

Catherine Friedly, wife of John Friedly, dau of late Abraham Huey, b. Jan 7, 1778, d. Sep 29, 1810, bur. Oct 1, 1810. Left husband, 3 sons and 2 daus.

Margaret Henning, dau of Jacob Hening and wife, Magdalene, b. Apr 24, 1778, d. Nov 11, 1810, bur. Nov 13, 1810.

Maria Magdalene Gundy, b. ca 1738, d. Nov 20, 1810, bur. Nov 21, 1810.

Elizabeth McElvain, wife of John McElvain, b. Sep 18, 1787, d. Dec 9, 1810, bur. Dec 10, 1810. Left husband and 1 dau.

Dr. John Luther, b. spring, 1757, d. Jan 28, 1811, bur. Jan 29, 1811. Left 3 sons and 1 dau.

Margaret Klein, wife of Christian Klein nee Schaeffer, b. ab. 36-37 years, d. Jun 6, 1811, bur. Jun 8, 1811. Left sad widower and 5 helpless children.

Jane Loyer, wife of Philip Loyer, b. May 8, 1780, d. May 19, 1811, bur. May 20, 1811.

Philip Eglee, b. May 22, 1757, d. Jun 17, 1811, bur. Jun 19, 1811.

Christian Schlichting, printer, b. in Holstein Germany ca 1771, d. Nov 5, 1811 age 40, bur. Nov 6, 1811.

Anna Maria Ott, widow of late Nicholas Ott, b. ca 1749, d. Nov 19, 1811 age 62, bur. Nov 20, 1811. Left 1 son and 1 dau.

Magdalene Heiss, wife of Jacob Heiss, dau of John Schneider, b. Mar 26, 1784, m. Dec 18, 1810, d. Jan 16, 1812, bur. Jan 18, 1812. Left a young widower and a new born.

Philip Peiffer, b. ca 1777, d. Feb 7, 1812 age 35, bur. Feb 9, 1812. Left widow and 2 young children.

Christian Blasser, b. ca 1761, d. Feb 10, 1812 age 41, bur. Feb 12, 1812.

John Peter Bayer, b. Jan 1, 1771, m. Mar 19, 1793, d. Feb 20, 1812, bur. Feb 22, 1812. Left a widow.

Susanna Schaeffer nee Braun, wife of William Schaeffer, b. Sep 18, 1790, m. May 5, 1811, d. Mar 17, 1812, bur. Mar 19, 1812. Left husband and new born child.

Lydia Kelker, wife of Fredeick Kelker, dau of Carl Gemberling and wife Maria, b. Apr 9, 1786, m. Aug 31, 1806, d. May 2, 1812, bur. May 3, 1812.

Juliana Yontz nee Mayer, wife of Jacob Yontz, b. Aug 3, 1777, d. Jun 14, 1812, bur. Jun 15, 1812. Left husband and young dau.

Susanna Wetherholdt nee Witman, widow of late Carl Wetherholdt, b. Jun 15, 1730 in Canton, Zurich, d. Aug 10, 1812, bur. Aug 11, 1812. Left son and 2 daus.

Mary Durang, wife of John C. Durany [Durang], b. ca 1768, d. Sep 1, 1812 age 44, bur. Sep 2, 1812. A comedian in Philadelphia Theatre, died while on tour. *(Char Durang, the son made the art. The pastor got the initials mixed. She d. while the company was on tour in Europe.)*

Henry Brunner, b. spring 1749, d. Sep 14, 1812, bur. Sep 15, 1812. Left widow, 3 sons and 3 dau.

John Easton, b. ca 1759, d. Sep 20, 1812 age 53, bur. Sep 22, 1812 in the English cemetery.

John Schiffer, b. Feb 20 1742, m. Christine Leinbach in 1772, bur. Oct 20, 1812. Left 3 sons and 4 daus.

Anna Maria Braun dau of Melchior Braun and wife Maria, b. Jan 26, 1785, d.Nov 15, 1812, bur. Nov 16, 1812.

John Duncan Campbell, b. Jun 10, 1768, (m. Barbara Waifield May 13, 1793), d. Mar 11, 1813, bur. Mar 12, 1813.

Sebastian Schneider, b. May 19, 1775, (m. Elizabeth Young, Apr 9, 1812), d. Jun 13, 1813, bur. Jun 15, 1813.

Samuel Peffer, son of late George Peffer and wife, Susanna, now Mrs. Ferree, b. Jun 5, 1798, d. Aug 11, 1813, bur. Aug 12, 1814.

Catherine Scarlet, widow of late Henry Scarlet, dau of late Henry Brunner, b. Sep 29, 1782, d. Oct 28, 1813, bur. Oct 30, 1813 at Trindel's Church, Cumberland County. Left 4 children.

Jacob Miller, b. Feb 12, 1779 or 1780, (m. Maria Semer), d. Dec 16, 1813, bur. Dec 17, 1813. Left a widow.

Maria Rosina Hertz, wife of Ludwig Hertz, dau of ---- Rhein, b. Jan 10, 1762, d. Mar 1, 1814, bur. Mar 4, 1814. Left a widower and 6 children.

REFORMED CHURCH, HUMMELSTOWN

[Following 1796-1798 Baptisms by Rev. Ludwig Lupp.]

Wilhelm of Johannes and Catharina Bretz, b. Mar 16, 1796; bapt. Apr 23, 1796. Spon: Parents.

Johannes of Peter Bük and Elisabeth, b. Mar 11, 1796; bapt. (same day). Spon: Johan Heinrich Stentz and Elisabeth.

Elia of Johannes Fox and Margereth, b. Mar 24, 1796; bapt. Jun 19, 1796. Spon: parents.

Maria Ester of Martin Schell and Catharina, b. Mar 4, 1796; bapt. Jun 19, 1796. Spon: Johan Pathenar and Ester.

Elisabeth of Demÿ and Anna, b. Mar 29, 1796; bapt. Jun 19, 1796. Spon: Mathàis Wolf and Anna Maria.

Anna Maria of Heinrich Hahn and Christina, b. Jul 27, 1796; bapt. Aug 14, 1796. Spon: Heinrich Schmitt and Anna Maria.

David of Heinrich Alleman and Julianna, b. Apr 27, 1796; bapt. Aug 14, 1796. Spon: Parents.

Tobias of Johannes Seÿbert and Elisabeth, b. Aug 13, 1796; bapt. Sep 9, 1796. Spon: Elisabeth Seÿbert.

Sarah of Adam Stamm and Catharina, b. Jan 4, 1797; bapt. Mar 20, 1797. Spon: parents.

Jacob Christian Demmÿ and Anna, b. Apr 7, 1797; bapt. May 21, 1797. Spon: parents.

Sussanna of Robert Dunbar and Magdalena, b. Jun 22, 1797; bapt. Jul 16, 1797. Spon: parents.

Jacob of Philip Fisborn and Anna Maria, b. Mar 31, 1797; bapt. Jul 16, 1797. Spon: Parents.

Jacob of Heinrich Baumgartner and Elisabeth, b. Apr 29, 1797; bapt. Jul 16, 1797. Spon: Parents.

Maria Magdalena of Christian Ludwig and Anna Maria, b. Aug 17, 1796; bapt. Jul 16, 1797. Spon: parents.

Catharina Elisabetha of Micheal Leim(?) and Elisabeth, b. Jul 12, 1797; bapt. Jul 16, 1797. Spon: Elisabeth Bretz.

Johan Heinrich of Johannes Bichler and Elisabeth, b. Apr 2, 1797; bapt. Jul 16, 1797. Spon: Heinrich Krumm (Kremm?) and Anna Maria.

Elisabeth of Johan Seÿbert and Elisabeth, b. Feb 6, 1798; bapt. Apr 20, 1798. Spon: Elisabeth Seÿbert.

Jacob of Peter Bük and Elisabeth, b. Oct 8, 1798; bapt. Aug 20, 1798. Spon: Christian Frank.

Thomas of Thomas James and Catharina, b. Dec 25, 1797; bapt. Mar 19, 1978. Spon: Magdalena Bretz.

Barbara of Philip Oberkirsch and Elizabeth, b. Nov 3, 1797; bapt. Mar 20, 1798. Spon: Barbara Härman.

Anna Maria of Heinrich Weber and Magdalena, b. Mar 19, 1798; bapt. Jun 13, 1798. Spon: Anna Maria Weber.

Maria of Christian Böhm and Barbara, b. Jun 22, 1797; bapt. Dec 7, 1811.

Barbara (wife of Frederick Rudy) of Christian Huffer and Regina, b. Nov 15, 1778; bapt. Dec 7, 1811.

BURIALS

Catharina Baum, widow of Johannes, b. Nov 9, 1776; d. Oct 15, 1808; bur. Oct 17, 1808.

David Eckstein, schullehrer, 50 y; bur. Feb 15, 1809.

Fridrich Blessing, b. Aug 27, 1759; d. Mar 2, 1809; bur. Mar 3, 1809. Leaving a widow, 1 son and 6 daus; bur. Mar 3, 1809.

George Toot, b. Dec, 1792; d. 3/1/1810; bur. Mar 3, 1810.

Geo. Louer, Esq., b. 9/15/1753; d. 12/29/1810; bur. Dec 30, 1810. Left widow and 8 children.

Johan Fischer of Johan and Anna Maria, b. May 3, 1796; d. Mar 6, 1811; bur. Mar 7, 1811.

SHOOP'S REFORMED CHURCH RECORDS

Henry of Lorenze and Magdalena Hypsher, b. Oct, 1782; bapt. May 1783. Spon: Christopher Shupp and wife, Rosina.

Anna Maria of Philip and Maria Schmidt; b. Apr 19, 1793; bapt. May, 1783. Spon: Spon: Christopher Shupp and wife, Rosina.

John of Christopher and Rosina Shupp, b. May 15, 1771; bapt. Jun 5, 1771. Spon: John Parthemore and wife, Catharine.

Daniel of Christopher and Rosina Shupp, b. Feb 15, 1774; bapt. Mar 3, 1774. Spon: Christopher Shupp and wife, Margaret.

Catharine of Christopher and Rosina Shupp, b. Sep 12, 1775; bapt. Nov 3, 1774. Spon: John Shoop and Catharine Blessly, both single.

Jacob of Christopher and Rosina Shupp, b. Feb 10, 1778; bapt. Mar 7, 1778. Spon: John Parthemore and wife, Catharine.

Jacob of John Adam and Magdalena Loefle, b. May 1, 1783; bapt. Jun 18, 1783. Spon: Jacob Meyer and wife, Barbara.

Christopher of Philip and Ann Eve Parthemore, b. Jun 17, 1783; bapt. Jun 19, 1783. Spon: John Parthemore and wife, Catharine.

John Adam of Frederick and Catharine Schweitzer, b. May 23, 1783; bapt. Jun 9, 1783. Spon: Thomas Mohr and wife, Barbara.

Christiana of Barnhard and Christiana Folt, b. Jul 28, 1782; bapt. Nov 1782.

Elizabeth of John and Catharine Fritz. b. Aug 17, 1783; bapt. Oct 7, 1783. Spon: John Dietz and Elisabeth Pancake.

Elizabeth of Christopher and Rosina Shupp, b. Nov 9, 1783; bapt. Dec 7, 1783. Spon: Martin Shell and Catharine Parthemore, both single.

Conrad of Peter and Barbara Bobb, b. Jun. 12, 1780; bapt. Sep 10, 1780. Spon: Conrad Bobb and wife, Eve.

John George of Henry and Juliann Meyer, b. Nov 24, 1783; bapt. Feb 22, 1784. Spon: George Shupp and wife, Louisa.

John George of Conrad and Eve Bobb, b. Dec 26, 1783; bapt. Mar 21, 1784.

Anna Christiana of John George and Magdalena Diefenbach, b. Dec 29, 1783; bapt. Mar 24, 1784. Spon: Joseph Keller and wife, Elizabeth.

John Peter of John and Barbara Moore, b. Jan 22, 1784; bapt. Mar 21, 1784. Spon: Frederick Schweitzer and wife, Catharine.

John Thomas of John and Barbara Moore, b. Mar 3, 1781; bapt. Mar 21, 1782. Spon: Frederick Schweitzer and wife, Catharine.

Spon: Frederick Schweitzer and wife, Catharine.

Anna Barbara Elizabeth of Henry Pohl and Margaret, b. Jan 25, 1784; bapt. Apr 18, 1784. Spon: John Gomsert and Fanny Pohl both single.

Anna Christiana of John Valentine Snyder and Elisabeth, b. Nov 18, 1783; b. bapt. Apr 19, 1784. Spon: John Tice and Christiana Schmidt, both single.

Christiana and Justina, twins of Michael Schmidt and Elizabeth, b. Mar 22, 1784; bapt. Apr 19, 1784. Spon: Jacob Hosinger and Cath. Schmidt, both single, and John Miller and wife, Margaret.

John Conrad of John Strock and Catharine, b. Sep 30, 1783; bapt. Apr, 1784. Spon: John Miller and wife, Margaret.

Maria Elizabeth of George Sheetz and Barbara, b. 1784; bapt. May 16, 1784.

Catharine of Michael Leim and Catharine, b. 1784; bapt. May 16, 1784. Spon: Jacob Meyers and wife, Barbara.

Barbara of Peter Eisenhower and Anna, b. Mar 9, 1784; bapt. May 16, 1784. Spon: John Shui and wife, Catharine.

Catharine of Michael Phillipi and Elisabeth, b. Apr 9, 1784; bapt. May 16, 1784. Spon: Peter Felty and wife, Catharine.

Anna of Henry Tittle and Magdalena, b. Mar 4, 1784; bapt. May 16, 1784. Spon: Peter Eisenhouer and wife, Anna.

Jacob of Vinton Reel and Phillipina, b. Mar 29, 1784; bapt. Aug 8, 1784. Spon: Jacob Whitmer.

John of John Martin and Regina, b. Jul 10, 1784; bapt. Aug 8, 1784. Spon: Henry Kistner and Barbara Bindnagle.

John of John Bobb and wife, b. Jan 25, 1784; bapt. Aug 8, 1784. Spon: Jacob Hosinger and Fanny Poling, both single.

Elizabeth of Thomas Kern and Sophia, b. Apr 6, 1785; bapt. May 16, 1785.

Christiana of John Strock and Catharine, b. Mar 6, 1782; bapt. May 16, 1785. Spon: Frederick Cassel and wife.

Elizabeth of Frederick Lennert and Maria, b. Apr 12, 1785; bapt. May 16, 1785. Spon: John Michael Felty and Elisabeth Brown.

Sabine of Jacob Toy (or Troye) and Barbara, b. Mar 3, 1785; bapt. May 16, 1785. Spon: Sabine Kisszen.

Catharine Susan of George Reinmaker and wife, b. Aug 5, 1784; bapt. May 16, 1785.

John of Philip Schmidt and Maria Agnes, b. Feb 21, 1784; bapt. May 16, 1785. Spon: Martin Shell and Catharine Parthemore.

Louisa of George Shupp, b. Jan 9, 1785; bapt. May 16, 1785. Spon: John Parthemore and Catharine Bobb.

John Frederick of Christopher Shupp and Rosina, b. Jul 14, 1785; bapt. Jul 24, 1785. Spon: John Martin Shell and wife, Catharine.

Anna Catharine of John Martin Shell and Catharine, b. Jul 28, 1786; bapt. Oct 10, 1786. Spon: John Parthemore and wife, Catharine.

Christiana of Peter Valentine, b. Jan 21, 1786; bapt. Oct 10, 1786.

Elizabeth of Michael Poorman and Anna Maria, b. Dec 1786; bapt. Apr 2, 1787. Spon: Maria Poorman.

Maria Salome of Jacob Fahrling and Maria Salome, b. Oct 19, 1786, b. Apr 2, 1787. Spon: Francis Albert and wife.

Maria Magdalena of Stofel Shupp and Rosina, b. Jul 23, 1787; bapt. Sep 3, 1787. Spon: John Parthemore and wife.

Catharine Elizabeth of Henry Meyers and Julia Ann, b. Sep 24, 1787; bapt. Oct 21, 1787. Spon: Henry Emerich and wife, Catharine Elisabeth.

Thomas of Martin Lingle and Elizabeth, b. Oct 7, 1787; bapt. Oct 21, 1787. Spon: Thomas Lingle and wife, Ann Maria.

Barbara of John Christian Wagner and Anna Maria, b. Oct 14, 1787; bapt. Mar 24, 1788.

Anna Maria, wife of Michael Poorman, b. May 20, 1766; bapt. May 24, 1788.

"A daughter is born Mar 31 and bapt. May 24, 1788, and received the name of Martha. Spon: Jacob Seiders and wife. (After the foregoing entries are the following, but no names of parents, except it be the sisters of Anna Maria Poorman, whoever she may have been.)

"Esther is b. Dec 1772; bapt. May 24, 1788.

"Anna is b. 1769; bapt. May 24, 1788.

"Elizabeth is b. Apr, 1764; bapt. May 24, 1788.

----, son of Casper Heinecke and Magdalena, b. Aug 17, 1788.

George of George Schmidt and Eve, b. Oct 16, 1788; bapt. Oct 26, 1778. Spon: Lorenze Schmidt and wife.

Maria Dora of Adam Baroff and Barbara, b. Dec 27, 1777; bapt. Jan 25, 1788.

Maria Barbara of Henry Meyer and Julia Ann, b. Dec 10, 1786.

John Henry of Henry Meyer and Julia Ann, b. Jan 27, 1790; bapt. May 9, 1790.

John Peter of Peter Eisenhower and Ann, b. Jan 4, 1790; bapt. Aug 22, 1790.

Christiana of Christopher Shupp and Rosina, b. May 4, 1791; bapt. Jun 13, 1791.

Catharine of Daniel Fehrling and Catharine, b. 1793. Spon: Jacob Fehrling and wife, Salome.

Catharine of William Lacksly and Anna Maria, b. Aug 27, 1793. Spon: George Hain and wife, Catharine.

John of Daniel Fehrling and Catharine, b. Sep 27, 1796; bapt. Dec 27, 1795. Spon: Mathias Wolf and wife, Anna Maria.

Anna Maria of Christian Walborn and Elisabeth, b. Jan 1, 1796; bapt. Feb 14, 1796.

John George of Jonas Groff and Elizabeth, b. Jan 5, 1796; bapt. Feb 26, 1796. Spon: Frederick Schweitzer and wife, Elizabeth.

John George of Mathias Schmidt and Barbara, b. Oct 27, 1795; bapt. May 1, 1796. Spon: Henry Schmidt and wife, Anna Maria.

John George of Michael Kunkle and Christiana, b. Mar 14, 1796; bapt. Aug 2, 1796. Spon: George Vogt and wife, Maria.

Samuel of John London and Kate, b. and ba. Mar 15, ----.

Maria Elizabeth of Daniel Poorman and Christiana, b. Jul 14, 1796. Spon: Jacob Beck and wife, Maria.

Peter of Philip Bobb and Gertrude, b. Nov 22, 1796; bapt. Dec 4, 1796. Spon: Peter Bobb and wife, Barbara.

Maria Magdalena of Philip Reel and Catharine, b. Nov 26, 1796; bapt. Jan, 1797. Spon: Philip Bobb and wife, Gertrude.

Rachael of John Beck and Barbara, b. Nov 30, 1796; bapt. Feb 5, 1797. Spon: Rachael Fackler.

Eva Catharine of Peter Poop (Bobb) and Elizabeth , b. Jan 23, 1797; bapt. Mar 5, 1797. Spon: Philip Reel and wife, Catharine.

John of George Snider and Catharine, b. Oct 22, 1796; bapt. Mar 5, 1797. Spon: John Snider and wife, Magdalena.

Maria Barbara of Jacob Keplinger and Barbara, b. Mar 1, 1797; bapt. Apr 2, 1797.

Benjamin of Casper Stoeber and Eve, b. Nov 24, 1796; bapt. Mar 15, 1797. Spon: Casper Stoeber, Jr. and wife, Barbara.

Maria Rosina of Lucas Lanekan and Catharine, b. Apr 22, 1797; bapt. May 14, 1797. Spon: Rosina Mayer.

Maria Pfannekuchen of Frederick Pancake and Catharine, b. Mar 14, 1797; bapt. Jun 18, 1797. Spon: Polly Poorman.

Christiana of Frederick Cassel and Christiana, b. Apr 20, 1797; bapt. Jun 18,1797. Spon: Christian Walborn and his wife, Elisabeth.

Mary Magdalena of Peter Scheile and Catharine, b. Jul --; bapt. Jul

16, 1797. Spon: George Scheile and wife Catharine.

Jacob of Thomas Kern and Catharine, b. May 1, 1797; bapt. Aug 6, 1797. Spon: Jacob Millisen and wife, Maria.

Maria Elizabeth of John Eisenhower and Catharine, b. Nov 3, 1797; bapt. Dec 3, 1797. Spon: Thomas Kalnat and wife, Elizabeth.

Maria Christiana of Martin Koch and Eve, b. Dec 24, 1797; bapt. Jan 4, 1798. Spon: Christiana Felty.

Maria Magdalena of Daniel Fehrling and Catharine, b. Dec 29, 1797; bapt. Apr 22, 1798. Spon: Magdalena Felty.

Abraham of Jacob Fehrling and Salome, b. Feb 4, 1798; bapt. May 22, 1798. Spon: Balthaser Alberthal.

Elizabeth of Philip Bobb and Gertrude, b. May 13, 1798; bapt. Jun 10, 1798. Spon: Elizabeth Stauch.

Jacob of Daniel Poorman and Christina, b. Jun 16, 1798; bapt. Jul 22, 1798. Spon: Jacob Keplinger and wife, Barbara.

Sarah of Michael Kunkle and Christiana, b. Jun 16, ----; bapt. Aug 26, 1798. Spon: Sarah Shupp.

Anna Maria of John Gaul and Anna Maria, b. Nov 20, 1797; bapt. Sep 23, 1798. Spon: John Beck and wife, Barbara.

Anna Maria of William Ewen and Christiana, b. Aug 28, 1798; bapt. Oct 21, 1798. Spon: Michael Wohlfarth and wife, Elizabeth.

Jacob of Philip Reem and Catharine, b. Sep 5, 1798; bapt. *[as mentioned]*. Spon: Jacob Stauch and wife, Catharine.

Sarah of Christian Walborn and Elizabeth, b. Jun 15, 1798; bapt. Sep 24, 1798.

John George of Henry Sherk and Elizabeth, b. Dec 24, 1798; bapt. Apr 21, 1799. Spon: Barbara Seider.

Maria Catharine of George Schultz and Maria, b. Feb 19, 1799; bapt. Apr 21, 1799. Spon: John Beck and wife, Maria.

Esther of Frederick Cassel and Christian, b. Nov 3, 1798; bapt. Jun 2, 1799. Spon: Henry Berry and wife, Esther.

John Jacob of Martin Schell and Catharine, b. Apr 4, 1799; bapt. Jun 1, 1799. Spon: Christopher Shupp and wife, Rosina.

John Casper of Casper Stoever and Eva, b. Mar 5, 1799; bapt. Jun 2, 1799. Spon: John Felty and Catharine Schupp.

John of Lucas Laneken and Catharine, b. Jun 13, 1799; bapt. Jul 14, 1799. Spon: John Meyer.

John Jacob of Peter Bobb and Elizabeth, b. Mar 15, 1799, bapt. [in same year or month]. Spon: Eva Margaret Bomberger.

Sarah of Philip Reel and Catharine, b. Jan 31 1799; bapt. *[as mentioned].* Spon: Barbara Bobb.

Jacob of Daniel Fehrling and Catharine, b. Feb 19, 1790; bapt. May 18, 1800. Spon: Martin Koch and wife, Eve.

Maria Elizabeth of John Garverich and wife Barbara, b. Apr 3, 1800; bapt. Aug 3, 1800. Spon: Philip Bobb and wife, Gertrude.

George of George Schultz and Maria, b. Oct 20, 1800; bapt. Feb 22, 1801. Spon: George Schultz and wife, Elizabeth.

Maria of Henry Sherk and Elizabeth, b. Nov 26, 1800; bapt. Jan 5, 1802.

WENERICH'S REFORMED CHURCH

Philip of John Gaul and Ana Maria, b. Aug 14, 1791. Spon: John Philip Heckert and Ana Maria.

Henry of Michael Walborn and Catharine, b. Nov 10, 1791. Spon: Henrich Walborn and Gerthlis Wenrich.

Christine of Conrad Schmidt and wife Catharine, b. Oct 6, 1791; bapt. Oct 21, 1791. Spon: parents.

Daniel of Conrad Schafer and wife Barbara, b. Jan 2, ----; bapt. Oct 21, ----. Spon: parents.

Elisabeth of Frantz Wenrich, b. Feb 2, 1793; bapt. Feb 10, 1793. Spon: Jonathan Beyer and wife Elizabeth.

---- of Peter Lenhart, b. Oct --, 1794; bapt. Oct 12, 1794. Spon: Frantz Wenrich and wife Elisabeth.

---- of Hannes Peter, b. Oct 12, 1794. Spon: Jacob Michel and wife Etwina.

John of John Lerch and Catherine, b. Oct 31, 1794; bapt. Nov 7, 1794. Spon: John Umberger and wife Margaret.

John George of ---- Brechtbill and Dorothy, b. Oct 31, 1794; bapt. Nov 7, 1794. Spon: George Feeser and wife Dorothy.

Christina of Daniel Porman and Christina, b. Oct 11, 1794. Spon: Henrich Kiblinger and Abalona.

John George of Killian Lang and Barbara, b. Aug 22, 1794; bapt. Jan 1, 1795. Spon: Michael Umberger and wife Maria.

Maria Magdalene of Martin Koch and Eva, b. Dec 21, 1794; bapt. Apr 6, 1795. Spon: Michael Walborn.

Gottlieb of Caspar Stover and Eva, b. Dec 12, 1794; bapt. Apr 26, 1795. Spon: Adam Koch.

John Jacob of Fred Schuy and Veronica, b. Aug 24, 1794; bapt. Apr 26, 1795. Spon: Daniel Panfenberg and wife Catherine.

Susan of George Reiter and Catharine Elizabeth, b. Dec 19, 1794. Spon: Gerthliis Umberger.

Jacob of Philip Witmer and Anna Maria, b. Apr 1, 1795. Spon: Stephen Rannels and Magdalene.

Catharine of Philip Gergerich and Margaret, b. Apr 3, 1795. Spon: Frantz Fuchs (Fox) and Catherine.

John of Jacob Watz(?) and Christine, b. Nov 22, 1794. Spon: Gottlieb Spohn and Catharine.

William of David David and Christina, b. Dec 2, 1794. Spon: William Hennson and Catharine.

Elizabeth of Joseph Umberger and Margaret, b. Jul 2, 1795. Spon: Frantz Wenrich and wife Elisabeth [hand written].

Elizabeth of Jonathan Bayer and Elizabeth, b. Jul 3, 1795. Spon: Michael Walborn and Catharine.

Samuel of William Berly and Anna Maria, b. Oct 4, 1795. Spon: Philip Heckert and Maria.

John of Richard Gald and Catharine, b. Jan 13, 1796. Spon: Rudolph Boihr and Anna Eva.

Maria Elizabeth of George Focht and Maria, b. Jan 6, 1796. Spon: Philip Heckert and Anna Maria.

Margaret of Michael Walborn and wife Elizabeth, b. Jul, ---. Spon: Jonathan Beyer and wife.

Elizabeth of John Kiblinger and wife Elizabeth, b. Aug 18, 1796; bapt. Sep 26, 1796. Spon: Thomas Schmidt and wife Christiana.

John Jacob of George Tschuty and Eva, b. Nov 3, 1796; bapt. Feb 12, 1797. Spon: Jacob ---- and his wife.

Elizabeth of William Jensen and wife Catharine, b. Nov 29, ----; bapt. Feb 12, ----. Spon: Jonathan Bayer and wife.

Sara Susanna of Gotleib Spohn and Catharine, b. Jul 2, 1797. Spon: Michael Walborn and wife, and Peter Wenrich.

Johannes of Henry Fitting, b. Jun 1, 1797; bapt. Jul 2, 1797. Spon: John ---- and wife.

Sarah of Adam Hahn and wife Eva, b. Jul 30, ----. Spon: George Schmitt and Eva.

Elizabeth of Jacob Sherrick and wife Catharine, b. Apr 8, ----; bapt. May 14, 1799. Spon: Peter Heckert and wife Elizabeth.

John Solomon of Peter Velte (Felty) and Christina, b. Feb 27 ----; bapt. Jul 14, 1799. Spon: parents.

Catharine of George Becker and wife Elizabeth, b. Dec 7, 1798; bapt. Aug 28, 1799. Spon: Philip Reuter.

George of Philip Reuter and wife Catharine, b. May 10 ----; bapt. same day. Spon: Caspar Hinckel and wife Magdalena.

John Jacob of Philip Gerberick and wife Margaret, b. Apr 3 ----; bapt. Oct 5, 1799. Spon: George Gerberick and wife Hanna.

Jacob of John Bucher and wife Elizabeth, b. Sep 9, ----; bapt. Oct 6, 1799. Spon: Jacob Bucher and Eva Plauck.

Elizabeth of Peter Wenrich and wife Susana, b. Sep 8, ----; bapt. same day. Spon: Frank Wenerich and wife Elizabeth.

David of John Eisenhauer and wife Catharine, b. Sep 9, ----; bapt. same day. Spon: Conrad Frey and wife Elizabeth.

John Peter and John George Schmidt and wife Eva, b. Aug 1, ----; bapt. same day. Spon: Michel Bartholome.

Elizabeth of Peter Weiss and wife Elizabeth, b. Dec 1, ----; bapt. Dec 9, 1799. Spon: John Jacob Conrad and wife Annamaria.

Annamaria of John Gergerich and wife Catharine, b. Oct 22, 1790; bapt. Mar 30, 1800. Spon: Barbara Kohr.

Henry of Peter Grum and Eva, b. Apr 17, 1791; bapt. ----. Spon: Henrich Schuy and Annamaria.

Henry of Peter Grum and Eva, b. Nov 7, 1795; bapt. ----. Spon: George Schelly and wife.

John of Peter Krum and Eva, b. Dec 16, 1798; bapt. ----. Spon: Henry Meyer and Elizabeth.

Susanna Christiana of John George Pfrenner and Elizabeth, b. Dec 6, 1799; bapt. Apr 11, 1800. Spon: Peter Krum and Eva.

[John of John Nicholas Conrad and wife Maria Margaret, b. Aug 23, ----; bapt. same day. Spon: John Jacob Conrad and wife Anna Maria.] handwritten

Eva Elizabeth of Adam Hahn and wife Eva, b. Feb 5, 1800; bapt. Apr 11, ----. Spon: Thomas Wenrich and wife Anna Maria.

Samuel of Jonathan Byer and Elizabeth, b. Apr, ----; bapt. May 30, 1800. Spon: parents.

Jacob of Johannes Kiblinger and Elizabeth, b. Mar 7, ----; bapt. Jun 22, 1800. Spon: Thomas Schmitt and Christina.

AnnaMaria of Paul Lingel and Ann Marie, b. Jun 26, ----; bapt. Jul 29, 1800. Spon: AnnaMaria Lingel.

Catharine of John Michael and wife Elizabeth, b. Jun 11, ----; bapt. Aug 3, 1800. Spon: Sarah Michael.

Elizabeth of Jonas Grist and Elisabeth, b. Aug 19, ----; bapt. Sep 28, 1800. Spon: Julian Meier.

Henry of John Fitting and wife Elizabeth, b. Jun 7, ----; bapt. same day. Spon: John Purman and wife Margaret.

Christina Elizabeth of Michael Schmitt and wife Anna, b. Jul 19, ----; bapt. same day. Spon: Thomas Schmitt and wife Elisabeth.

John of John Purmann and wife Margaret, b. Aug 1, ----; bapt. same day. Spon: John Fitting and wife Elizabeth.

Mar Barbara of Daniel Pornman and Christina, b. May 30 ----; bapt. Oct 12, 1800. Spon: Bar Kiblinger, single.

John Henry of Henry Fitting and wife AnnaMaria, b. Sep 10 ----; bapt. Oct 20, 1800. Spon: parents.

Maria Margaretta of William Ervin and wife Christina, b. Sep 11 ----;

bapt. Oct 20, 1800. Spon: Nicholas Conrad and wife Maria.

Maria Margaret of Philip Wittmeyer and wife Annamaria, b. Nov 22 - ---; bapt. Mar 1, 1801. Spon: A. Maria Conrad.

Henry of George Reiter and Catharine, b. Aug 27, 1800; bapt. Mar 31, 1801. Spon: John Schuy and Rebecca.

Ann Catharine of Daniel Schuy and Ann Catharine, b. Dec 28, 1800; bapt. Mar 31, 1801. Spon: Michael Meyer and Ann Catharine.

Salome of Jacob Schuy and Catharine, b. Jun 7, 1800; bapt. Mar 31, 1801. Spon: parents.

Elizabeth of Conrad Green and wife Elizabeth, b. Nov 26, 1800; bapt. May 3, 1801. Spon: Maria Magdalene Hinkel.

A. Catharine of Jacob Schnell and Mar Barbara, b. Dec 14, 1800; bapt. Jun 14, 1801. Spon: A. Maria Lentz.

ZION (KLINGER'S) CHURCH

Johen George of George Klinger and wife, Elisabeth, b. Sep 16, bapt. Sep 16, 1787. Spon: Joh. George Brosius.

Abraham of Adam Schwartz and wife, Rosina, b. Aug 15, 1777, bapt. Sep 16, 1787. Spon: Christian Stutzman.

Isaak of Adam Swarrtz and wife, Rosina, b. Sep 12, 1779, bapt. Sep 16, 1787. Spon: George Dieterich.

Sara of Adam Schwartz and wife, Rosina, b. May 2, 1781, bapt. Sep 16, 1787: Spon: Barbara Dieterich.

Elizabeth of Adam Schwartz, b. May 2, 1783, bapt. Sep 16, 1787: Spon: Elizabeth Stutzman.

Michael of Adam Schwartz and wife Rosina, b. May 4, 1787; bapt. Sep 16, 1787. Spon: Michael Burckert.

Adam of Adam Schwartz and wife, Rosina, b. May 4, 1787, bapt. Sep 16, 1787. Spon: Johan Fischer.

Joh. George of Johannes Bechtel and wife, Barbara, b. Jun 1; bapt. Sep 16, 1787. Spon: George Klinger.

Joh. Henrich of Phillip Kunzleman and wife, Cath., b. Nov 12, 1786, bapt. Sep 16, 1787; Spon: Henrich Furst and wife, Cath.

Michael of Michael Burckert and wife, Elisab., b. Jun 13, 1785, bapt. Sep 16, 1787. Spon: The parents.

Magdalena of Michael Burckert and wife, Elisab., b. Aug 15, 1786, bapt. Sep 16, 1787. Spon: Joh. Adam Schleich.

Joh. Nicholaus of Adam Hetherick and wife, Mary, b. Mar 4, 1789, bapt. Mar 15, 1789. Spon: Joh. Nice. Brosius and wife, Maria.

Joh. Nicholaus of Abraham Brosius and wife, Cath., b. Apr 1; bapt. May 3, 1789. Spon: Grandparents.

Joh. Nicholaus of Johan Jacob Brosius and wife, Mary, b. Apr 17; bapt. May 3, 1789. Spon: John. Nicholaus Brosius and wife, A. Maria.

Friederich of Nicholas Bohner and wife, Maria, b. Jan 20; bapt. May 3, 1789. Spon: Friederich Heckert and wife, Appalone.

A. Catharina, of Philip Aman and wife, A. Elisabeth, b. Jul 11; bapt. Oct 14, 1787. Spon: Johann Fischer and Cath. Stutzmanin, single.

Eve Elizabeth of Johannes Dieterich and wife, Barbara, b. Sep 21; bapt. Oct 14, 1787. Spon: George Kulman and Elisabeth Keisen, single.

A son of George Klinger and wife, Elisabeth, b. Sep 6; bapt. Sep 16, 1787. Spon: George Brosius and wife, Catharina.

Elisabeth of Phillip Klinger and wife, A. Maria, b. Dec 8 1787, bapt. Jan 6, 1788. Spon: Christian Bayer and wife, Catharine.

Joh. Henrick of George Hoffman and wife, Suss., b. Jul 10, 1787, bapt. Mar 21, 1788. Spon: Christian Bayer and wife, Catharina.

(Maria) Barbara of Casp. Emrich and wife, Christina, b. May 6; bapt. May 25, 1788. Spon: Peter Klinger and Magd. Haakin, unmarried.

Sara of James Osman and wife, Marg., b. Feb 5; bapt. May 25, 1788. Spon: Allexander Klinger and Magdalena Riedin, unmarried.

Abraham of Nicholas Schneider and wife, A. Maria, b. Sep 5; bapt. Oct 19, 1788. Spon: Abraham Brosius and wife, Catharina.

Jacob of Johannes Harter, Jr. and wife, A. Maria Elisabeth, b. Sep 6; bapt. Oct 19, 1788. Spon: Jacob Stauch and wife, Cath.

Joh. Thomas of Israel Ritter and wife, A. Maria, b. Dec 29, 1787, bapt. Oct 19, 1788. Spon: Christian Bayer and wife, Cath.

Jonathan of Jacob Stauch and wife, Cath., b. Nov 29; bapt. Dec 20, 1788. Spon: Hen. Trautman and Regi. (Regina) Toschoppen, unmarried.

Benjamin of Conrath Schreckengast and wife, Suss., b. Nov 15; bapt. Dec 20, 17888. Spon: Henrich Greninger and wife, A. Maria.

Jacob of Peter Schmidt and wife, A. Maria, b. Nov 28, 1788; bapt. Jan 19, 1789. Spon: Jacob Hehn and wife, Magdalene.

Appalona of Phillip Aman and wife, A. Elisabeth, b. Jan 30; bapt. Feb 15 1789. Spon: Peter Klinger and Hanna Colmein, unmarried.

Hon. Peter of Phillip Kuntzelman and wife, Cath., b. Oct 30, 1786, bapt. May 3, 1789. Spon: Peter Klinger and Barbara Kuntzelmannin, unmarried.

Catharina of Henrich Keiss and wife, Elisabeth, b. Apr 5; bapt. May 3, 1789. Spon: Christian Bayer and wife, Catharina.

Elisabeth of Jacob Harter and wife, Elisabeth, b. May 9; bapt. May 24, 1789. Spon: Andreas Harter and Elisabeth Kissingerin, unmarried.

M. Magdalena of Andreas Hoffman and wife, Margareth, b. May 27; bapt. Jun 28, 1789. Spon: M. Maagd. Umholsin.

Peter of George Klinger and wife, Elisabeth, b. Aug 14; bapt. Aug 23, 1789. Spon: Peter Klinger, unmarried.

M. Magdalena of George Dieterich and wife, A. Maria, b. Jun 11; bapt. Aug 23, 1789. Spon: A. Maria Keissin, unmarried.

R. Barbara of Michael Rissinger and wife, Christina, b. Sep 8; bapt. Oct 18, 1789. Spon: Hannah Kuhlmennin, unmarried.

Abraham of Jacob Hoffman and wife, Cath., b. Sep 20; bapt. Oct 18,

1789. Spon: Abraham Kissinger and wife.

M. Barbara of Joh. Adam Schleich and wife, Magda, b. Sep 19; bapt. Oct 18, 1789. Spon: Freiderich Denger and Barbara Burckerin, unmarried.

Juliana of Israel Ritter and wife, Maria, b. Jul 5; bapt. Oct 18, 1789. Spon: Peter Klinger and Elisabeth Kissingern, unmarried.

Adam of Adam Schwartz and wife, Christina, b. Sep 27; bapt. Nov 22, 1789. Spon: Henrich Bohner and wife, Catharina.

Eva Elisabeth of Alexander Klinger and wife, Magd., b. Dec 21; bapt. Dec 27, 1789. Spon: Philip Klinger and wife, Eva Elisabeth, grandparents.

Johannes of Johannes Dieterich and wife, b. Dec 6; bapt. Dec 27, 1789. Spon: Johannes Keiss, unmarried.

Jacob of Henrich Feehss and wife, Cath., b. Nov 27; bapt. Dec 27, 1789. Spon: G. Jacob Kulman, unmarried.

M. Magdalena of Phillip Klinger and wife, A. Maria, b. Jan 16; bapt. Jan 24, 1790. Spon: Alexander Klinger and wife, Magdalena.

Elisabeth of George Heim and wife, Rosina, b. Nov 12, 1789, bapt. Jan 24, 1790. Spon: Jacob Harter and wife, Elisabeth.

Johannes of Jacob Asman and wife, M. Marg., b. Nov 28, 1789, bapt. Jan 24, 1790. Spon: the parents.

M. Catharina of Abraham Brosius and wife, Cath., b. Apr 25, bapt. May 16, 1790. Spon: Adam Hetterich and wife, Marigreth.

Adam of Conrath Purst and wife, Marg., b. Mar 27; bapt. May 16, 1790. Spon: Adam Schleich and wife, M. Margd.

Mar. Margreth of Henrich Bohner and wife, Cath., b. Feb 12; bapt. May 16, 1790. Spon: Michael Rissinger and wife, Christina.

Andreas of Johannes Schreckengast and wife, Cath., b. Mar 12; bapt. Jun 13, 1790. Spon: Andreas Härter and Elisabeth Kissingern, unmarried.

Alexander of Joh. Hen. Schreckengast and wife, Cath., b. Apr 14; bapt. Jun 13, 1790. Spon: Alexander Klinger and wife, Magdalena.

Johannes of George Witemeyer and wife, Cath., b. May 3; bapt. Jul 11, 1790. Spon: the parents.

M. Margareth of Casper Emrich and wife, Christina, b. Jul 14; bapt. Aug 8, 1790. Spon: Go. Hack and wife, the grandparents.

Christina of George Hoffman and wife, Elisabeth, b. Aug 6; bapt. Sep 5, 1790. Spon: Michael Rissinger and wife, Christina.

Maria Elisabeth of Jo. Nicholaus Brosius and wife, Maria, b. Sep 25; ba Nov 7, 1790. Spon: George Klinger and wife, Elisabeth.

Johan Nicolaus of Jo. Nicolaus Schneider and wife, A. Maria, b. May 5; bapt. Nov 7, 1790. Spon: Jo. Nicolaus Brosius and wife, A. Maria.

M. Elisabeth of Johannes Bessler and wife, Elisabeth, b. Oct 19; bapt. Nov 7, 1790. Spon: Elisabeth Schäferin.

Anna Catharina of Peter Hätterich and wife, Hanna, b. Aug 16; bapt. Nov 7, 1790. Spon: Jo. George Brosius and wife, Catharina.

George Adam of George Adam Klinger and wife, Elisabeth, b. Nov 10; bapt. Dec 26, 1790. Spon: Adam Hetherich and wife, M. Margd.

Elisabeth of Mary Hehin (sic) and wife, Elisabeth, b. Aug 23, bapt. Oct 3, 1790. Spon: Philip Klinger, Jr. and wife, A. Maria.

Johannes of Carl Kulman and wife, Barbara, b. Jan 26; bapt. Feb 13, 1791. Spon: Joh. Kulman and wife, Sussanna, grandparents.

Mara. Sara of Jacob Stauch and wife, Cath., b. Jan 23; bapt. Feb 13, 1791. Spon: George Trautman and wife, Elisabeth.

Elisabeth of Michael Artz and wife, Cath., b. Feb 13; bapt. Mar 13, 1791. Spon: Philip Artz and wife, Barbara.

Christian of Christian Grimm and wife, Magd., b. Oct 9, 1790; bapt. Apr 10, 1791. Spon: the parents.

Christoph of Adam Hederich and wife, Mar. Marg., b. Mar 3; bapt. Apr 10, 1791. Spon: Nico. Hederich and wife, A. Cath.

Hanna of G. Jacob Kulman and wife, Cath., b. Mar 17; bapt. Apr 10, 1791. Spon: Peter Stein and wife, Hanna.

Johannes of Peter Schmidt and wife, An. Maria, b. Mar 12; bapt. Apr 29, 1791. Spon: Carl Kulman and wife, Barbara.

Catharina of Israel Ritter and wife, Maria, b. Mar 2; bapt. May 8, 1791. Spon: Catharina Burgartin, unmarried.

Mar. Barbara of Phillip Artz and wife, Barbara, b. Jul 12; bapt. Jul 31, 1791. Spon: Phillip Kuntzleman and wife.

Jacob of Adam Hammacher and wife, Cath., b. Jun 8; bapt. Jun 31, 1791. Spon: Matthais Herter, unmarried.

Ma. Magdalena of Andr. Lasch and wife, Magd., b. Jul 2; bapt. Aug 28, 1791. Spon: Susanna Hähnin, unmarried.

Joh. George of Abraham Brosius and wife, Cath., b. Aug 21; bapt. Aug 28, 1791. Spon: Jo. George Brosius and wife, Cath.

Philip of Sam Bäyer and wife, Elisabeth, b. Jul 7; bapt. Aug 28, 1791. Spon: Philip Artz and wife, Barbara.

G. Jacob of Johannes Strohschneider and wife, M. Elisabeth, b. Aug 27; bapt. Oct 25, 1791. Spon: George Groninger and An. Maria Strohscheider, unmarried.

Anna Maria of Alexander Klinger and wife, Magd., b. Oct 9; bapt. Oct 23, 1791. Spon: Phillip Klinger, Jr. and wife, An. Maria.

Jo. Peter of Fredrich Dinger and wife, Barbara, b. Jun 13; bapt. Oct 23, 1791. Spon: Peter Dinger, a grandfather.

George of Phillip Aman and wife, Elisabeth, b. Sep 7; bapt. Nov 20, 1791. Spon: George Klinger and wife, Elisabeth.

Ge. Peter of George Trautman and wife, Elisabeth, b. Sep 19; bapt. Dec 18, 1791. Spon: Jacob Trautman and Barbara Ried, unmarried.

Anna Barbara of Johannes Härter and wife, Mar. Elisabeth., b. Jan 18; bapt. Feb 12, 1792. Spon: Anna Barbara Ried, unmarried.

Maria of Adam Schwartz and wife, Rosina, b. Dec 20, 1791; bapt. Feb 12, 1792. Spon: Christ Bäter and wife, Cath.

Joh. Michael of George Dieterich and wife, An. Maria, b. Sep 22, 1791; bapt. Feb 12, 1792. Spon: Michael Artz and wife Cath.

George of Johs. Dieterich and wife, Barbara, b. Jan 2; bapt. Feb 12, 1792. Spon: George Trautman and wife, Elisabeth.

Joh. Philip of Philip Klinger and wife, An. Maria, b. Mar 11; bapt. Apr 8, 1792. Spon: Phillip Leffler and wife, Cath.

Jacob of Henrich Trautman and wife, Regina, b. Jan 13; bapt. Apr 8, 1792. Spon: Jacob Troutman and Cath. Hahnin, unmarried.

Magd. Catharina, of Jacob Hähn and wife, Christ., b. Feb 22; bapt. Apr 8, 1792. Spon: Cath. Rissinger, unmarried.

Magdalena of Hen. Gröninger and wife, An. Maria, b. Jan 14; bapt. Apr 8, 1792. Spon: Conrad Schreckengast and wife, Suss.

Johannes of Conrad Schreckengast and wife, Suss, b. Aug 12, 1791; bapt. Apr 8, 1792. Spon: Hen. Schreckengast and wife, Catharina.

Phillip of Peter Klinger and wife, Catharina, b. Apr 20; bapt. May 6, 1792. Spon: Phillip Klinger and wife, Eva Elisabeth, grandparents.

Andreas of Johannes Heim and wife, An. Cath., b. Mar 31; bapt. May 6, 1792. Spon: Andr. Härter and wife, Magdalena.

Sussan Elisabeth of Mich. Rissinger and wife, Christ., b. May 16; bapt. Jun 3, 1792. Spon: Ge Hoffman and wife.

Ma. Elisabeth of Will Simey and wife, Marg., b. Mar 24; bapt. Jun 3, 1792. Spon: Elisabeth Stutzmenin.

M. Magdalena of Johs. Schreckengast and wife, An. Cath., b. Apr 6; bapt. Jun 3, 1792. Spon: Simon Schreman and wife.

M. Magdalena of Joh. Christ. Fried. Wagner and wife, A. Maria, b. Apr 4; bapt. Jul 1, 1792. Spon: Jac. Schroder and wife, M. Magd.

Joha. Jacob of Carl Kulman and wife, Barb., b. Jul 14; bapt. Jul 29,

1792. Spon: G. Jacob Kulman and wife, Catharina.

Catharina of Andreas Härtter and wife, Magd., b. Jul 1; bapt. Jul 29, 1792. Spon: Peter Klinger and wife, Cath.

Elisabeth of Conrad Weiser and wife, Elisabeth, b. Jun 4; bapt. Jul 29, 1792. Spon: George Klinger and wife, Elisabeth.

Eva Elisabeth of Adam Hetterich and wife, Marg., b. Aug 11; bapt. Sep 2, 1792. Spon: Peter Hetterich and wife, Hanna.

Joh. George of Fredeich Dinger and wife, M. Barbara, b. Aug 28; bapt. Sep 30, 1792. Spon: George Klinger and wife, Elisabeth.

Johannes of Hen. Huber and wife, Cath., b. Sep 27; bapt. Oct 28, 1792. Spon: Henr. Bohner and wife, Cath.

Catharina of Mich. Artz and wife, Cath., b. Aug 28; bapt. Oct 28, 1792. Spon: Mart. Koppenhafer and wife, Suss.

Joh. Willhelm of Johann Jacobs and wife, Cath., b. May 27; bapt. Oct 28, 1792. Spon: Marg. Simmi.

Sussanna of Casp. Emrich and wife, Christina, b. Nov 9; bapt. Dec 23, 1792. Spon: Mart. Koppenhäfer and wife, Suss.

M. Catharina of Adam Hammacher and wife, Cath., b. Dec 5; bapt. Dec 23, 1792. Spon: George Klinger and wife, Elisabeth.

Joh. Michael of Phillip Artz and wife, Barbara., b. Oct 20; bapt. Dec 23, 1792. Spon: Mich. Artz and wife, Catharina.

An. Maria of Abraham Brosius and wife, M. Cath., b. Dec 15; bapt. Dec 23, 1792. Spon: Johann Brosius and wife, An. Maria.

Joh. Peter of George Klinger and wife, Elisabeth, b. Jan 26; bapt. Apr 14, 1793. Spon: Peter Klinger and wife, Catharina.

Johannes of Joh. Conrath Dietz and wife, Marg., b. Feb 14; bapt. Apr 14, 1793. Spon: Johannes Dieterich and wife, M. Barbara.

Anna Maria of Johannes Strohschneider and wife, M. Elisabeth., b. May 24; bapt. Jul 7, 1793. Spon: Hen Gröninger and wife, A. Maria.

M. Christina of George Dieterich and wife, A. Maria, b. Mar 28; bapt. Jul 7, 1793. Spon: Jacob Hähn and wife, Christina.

Maria Catharine of Hen. Wolfe and wife, Eva, b. Jul 11; bapt. Aug 4, 1793. Spon: Abraham Kissinger and wife, Catharina.

Catharina of Alexander Klinger and wife, Magdalena, b. Jul 27; bapt. Aug 4, 1793. Spon: Alexander Klinger and wife, Magdalena.

Alexander of Philip Klinger and wife, Magdalena, b. Jun 4; bapt. Sep 1, 1793. Spon: Alexander Klinger and wife, M. Catharina.

M. Catharina of Jacob Hoffman and wife, Suss., b. (not given); bapt. Aug 4, 1793. Spon: Abraham Kissinger and wife, M. Catharina.

Sussanna of G. Jacob Kulman and wife, Catharina, b. Sep 1; bapt. Sep 29, 1793. Spon: Johannes Kulman and wife, Suss.

Michael of Henrich Bohner and wife, Cath., b. Sep 21; bapt. Oct 27, 1793. Spon: Michael Artz and wife, Catharina.

Johannes of Andreas Härter and wife, Magd., b. Oct 6; bapt. Oct 27, 1793. Spon: Matth. Härter and Christina Deiblerin, unmarried.

Ma. Magdalena of Michael Burckert and wife, b. (not given); bapt. Oct 27, 1793. Spon: An. Maria Jungin, unmarried.

Maria Catharina of Stephan Lasch and wife, Magdalena, b. Nov 15; bapt. Dec 22, 1793. Spon: Jacob Stanch and wife, Catharina.

Eva Elisabeth of Peter Klinger and wife, Catharina, b. Jan 16; bapt. Feb 16, 1794. Spon: Philip Klinger and wife, Eva Elisabeth, grandparents.

Catharina of Carl Kulman and wife, Barbara, b. Nov 13, 1793; bapt. Feb 16, 1794. Spon: Alexander Klinger and wife, Magdalena.

Eva Elisabeth of Conrath Schreckengast and wife, Suss., b. Mar 15; bapt. Apr 13, 1794. Spon: G. Heil and Eva Schermensen, unmarried.

Magdalena of Hen. Trautman and wife, Regina, b. Sep 11, 1793; bapt. Apr 13, 1794. Spon: Magd. Tschoppin.

Eva Maria of Philip Artz and wife, Barbara, b. Feb 13; bapt. Apr 13, 1794. Spon: George Dieterich and A. Maria.

Philipps of Johannes Dieterich and wife, M. Barbara, b. Mar 5; bapt. Apr 13, 1794. Spon: Christian Bäyer and wife, Christina.

Maria Catharina of Elias Boffington and wife, Elisabeth, b. Oct 10, 1793; bapt. May 11, 1794. Spon: Abr. Kissinger and wife, M. Cath.

Salome of Nicholaus Jund and wife, Dorath, b. Apr 28; bapt. May 11, 1794. Spon: Alexander Klinger and wife, Magd.

Eva Elisabeth of Hen. Peehss and wife, Cath., b. Jun 17, 1793; bapt. May 11, 1794. Spon: Phillip Klinger and wife, Eva Elisabeth.

Matheias of Johannes Härter and wife, M. Elisabeth, b. Jun 7; bapt. Jun 8, 1874. Spon: Mathas Harter and M. Barbara Reidin, unmarried.

Maria Magdalena of Adam Hammacher and wife, M. Cath., b. Mar 27; bapt. Jun 8, 1794. Spon: Barbara Strohschnitterin.

Joseph of George Trautman and wife, Elisabeth, b. Oct 8, 1793; bapt. Jun 8, 1794. Spon: Hannes Keiss, unmarried.

Johannes of Phillip Klinger and wife, An. Maria, b. Aug 3; bapt. Sep 7, 1794. Spon: the grandparents.

Wilhelm of Anna Bellis, b. Apr 20, 1784; bapt. Sep 7, 1794. Spon:

Mrs. Elisabeth Asmennin.

Johann Martin of Joh. Martÿ and wife, Elisabeth, b. Aug 27; bapt. Oct 25, 1795. Spon: Peter Stein and wife, Hanna.

Barbara of Daniel Jund and wife, An. Maria, b. Nov 28, 1794 bapt. Oct 25, 1795. Spon: Carl Kulman and wife, Barbara.

Friederich of Philip Geress and wife, An. Maria, b. Nov 26, 1794; bapt. Oct 25, 1795. Spon: Andreas Scheth and wife, Elisabeth.

Johan Philip of George Klinger and wife, Elisabeth, b. Oct 2; bapt. Oct 25, 1795. Spon: Jo. Philip Klinger and wife, An. Maria.

Anna Catharina of G. Jacob Kulman and wife, Cath., b. Aug 27; bapt. Oct 25, 1795. Spon: Carl Kulman and wife, Barbara.

Barbara of George Dieterich and wife, An. Maria, b. Apr 23; bapt. Oct 25, 1795. Spon: Philip Artz and wife, Barbara.

Regina of Carl Kulman and wife, Barbara, b. Aug 6; bapt. Oct 25, 1795. Spon: Peter Stein and wife, An. Maria.

Johan Peter of Peter Klinger and wife, Catharina, b. Jan 2; bapt. Apr 3, 1796. Spon: Philip Klinger and wife, An. Maria.

Catharina of Peter Schmidt and wife, A. Maria, b. Oct 17, 1795; bapt. Apr 3, 1796. Spon: George Kulman and wife, Catharina.

Alexander of Casp. Emrich and wife, Christ., b. Nov 24, 1795; bapt. Apr 3, 1796. Spon: Alexander Klinger and wife, Magd.

Barbara of Johannes Eder and wife, Barbara, b. Feb 4; bapt. Apr 3, 1796. Spon: Philip Artz and wife, Barbara.

Philip of Philip Artz and wife, Barbara, b. Nov 6, 1795; bapt. Apr 3, 1796. Spon: Andreas Schropp and wife, Cath.

Johan Henrich of Hen. Bohner and wife, Cath.; b. Dec 16, 1795; bapt. Apr 3, 1796. Spon: Andreas Schropp and wife, Cath.

Elisabeth of Peter Schmidt and wife, Christina, b. Sep 16; bapt. Sep 26, 1796. Spon: Peter Schmidt and wife, Anna Maria.

Johann Peter of Philip Klinger and wife, An. Maria, b. Jun 1; bapt. Apr 8, 1797. Spon: Peter Klinger and wife, Cath.

Emie of Gideon Williamson and wife, Eva Elisabeth, b. Mar 15; bapt. Apr 18, 1797. Spon: Hen. Stehner and wife, Catharina.

Johannes of Ge. Adam Klinger and wife, An. Elisabeth, b. Mar 29; bapt. Apr 18, 1797. Spon: Johan Klinger and wife, Elisabeth.

Joh. Peter of Johan Kuntzelman and wife, Marg., b. Feb 11; bapt. Apr 18, 1797. Spon: Peter Stein and wife, Hanna.

Catharina of Jacob Trautman and wife, Maria, b. Jan 29; bapt. May 14, 1797. Spon: Catharina Klinger, unmarried.

Magdalena of Johannes Strohschneider and wife, M. Elisabeth, b. Feb

24; bapt. May 14, 1797. Spon: Peter Belin and wife.

Catharina of Peter Ritzman and wife, Cath. Elisabeth, b. Feb 12; bapt. May 14, 1797. Spon: Friederich Dubentorf and wife, Anna.

Sara of Thomas Asman and wife, Elisabeth, b. Dec 24, 1796; bapt. May 14, 1797. Spon: Peter Klinger and wife, Catharina.

Daniel of Raberd Asman and wife, Magd., b. Dec 16, 1797; bapt. May 14, 1797. Spon: George Kissinger and Magd. Forry, single.

Johannes of Jacob Hähn and wife, Christina, b. May 23; bapt. Jun 11, 1797. Spon: Friederich Häberling and wife, Catharina.

Elisabeth of Casper Emrich and wife, Christina, b. Sep 9; bapt. Oct 29, 1797. Spon: And. Schäd and wife, Elisabeth.

Alexander of Alexander Klinger and wife, Magd., b. Sep 16; bapt. Oct 29, 1797. Spon: Alexander Klinger, unmarried.

Christina of Conrad Weiser and wife, Elizabeth, b. Jul 31; bapt. Oct 29, 1797. Spon: Alexander Klinger and wife, Magdalena.

Johan George of Peter Klinger and wife, Catharina, b. Jan 7; bapt. Feb 23, 1798. Spon: George Klinger and wife, Elisabeth.

Catharina of Rabert Asman and wife, Magdalena, b. Feb 10; bapt. Jul 5, 1799. Spon: Elisabeth Bahna.

Joh. George of Martin Farringer and wife, Elisabeth, b. Jun 22; bapt. Jul 6, 1799. Spon: Joh. Sallade and wife, Margaretha.

Leonard of Johannes Dieterich and wife, M. Barbara, b. Jun 1; bapt. Jul 6, 1799. Spon: Peter Schmidt and wife, A. Maria.

Joh. George of George Hollenbach and wife, Susanna, b. Jun 18; bapt. Jul 6, 1799. Spon: Martin Farringer and wife, Elisabeth.

Jacob of Christian Hähn and wife, Elisabeth, b. May 25; bapt. Jul 6, 1799. Spon: Jacob Hähn and wife, Christina.

Peter of Carl Kulman and wife, Barbara, b. Jul 25; bapt. Aug 18, 1799. Spon: Andreas Sched and wife, Elisabeth.

Christina of George Grob and wife, Salome, b. Tuesday after Whit Sunday; bapt. Aug 18, 1799. Spon: Johannes Bessler and wife, Elisabeth.

Johannes of Elias Boffenton and wife, Elisabeth, b. May 28; bapt. Aug 18, 1799. Spon: Johannes Kissinger, unmarried.

Susanna of Martin Koppenhafer and wife, Sussanna, b. Aug 17; bapt. Sep 29, 1799. Spon: Peter Stein and wife, Hanna.

Elisabeth of Philip Artz and wife, Barbara, b. Aug 18; bapt. Sep 29, 1779. Spon: Joh. Kuntzelman and wife, Marg.

Alexander of G. Adam Klinger and wife, Elisabeth, b. Aug 25; bapt. Sep 29, 1799. Spon: Alexander Klinger and wife, Magd.

Leonard of Adam Hetterich and wife, M. Marg., b. Jan 19; bapt. Mar 16, 1800. Spon: Leonard Emrich and wife, Julianna.

Elisabeth of George Kulman and wife, Catharina, b. Feb 23; bapt. Mar 16, 1800. Spon: Andreas Sched and wife, Elisabeth.

Juliana of Friederich Kreutzer and wife, Julianna, b. Nov 15, 1799; bapt. Mar 16, 1800. Spon: Peter Stein and wife, Hanna.

Daniel of Daniel Jund and wife, Anna Maria, b. Aug 11, 1799; bapt. Mar 16, 1800. Spon: Andreas Sched and wife, Elisabeth.

Joh. George of Jacob Asman and wife, Marg., b. Nov 22, 1799; bapt. Aug 10, 1800. Spon: Joh. George Ridt, unmarried.

Joh. Jacob of Alexander Klinger and Magd., b. Jul 17; bapt. Aug 10, 1800. Spon: George Kulman and wife, Catharine.

Catharina of Peter Schmidt, Jr. and wife, Christina, b. Aug 25; bapt. Nov 30, 1800. Spon: George Kulman and wife, Catharina.

Catharina of Phillip Riedt and wife, Catharina, b. Aug 24; bapt. Nov 30, 1800. Spon: James Asman and wife, Marg.

M. Catharina of Johannes Kuntzelman and wife, Marg., b. Jul 22; bapt. Nov 30, 1800. Spon: Cath. Phees, unmarried.

Mally of Johan Rissinger and wife, Christina, b. Sep 25; bapt. Nov 30, 1800. Spon: Marg. Rissingerin, unmarried.

Christina of George Farringer and wife, Christina, b. Sep 5; bapt. Nov 30, 1800. Spon: Joh. Dessler and wife, Elisabeth.

Catharina of Joh. Schwalm and wife, Otilia Magd., b. Sep 27; bapt. Nov 30, 1800. Spon: Magd. Stutzmennin.

George of Joh. George Lowe and wife, Magdalena, b. Oct 7; bapt. Nov 30, 1800. Spon: Alexander Klinger and wife, Magd.

George of Jacob Wagoner and wife, Cath., b. Apr 10; bapt. Nov 30, 1800. Spon: George Dieterich and wife, Maria.

Sara of Jacob Gehres and wife, Elisabeth, b. Oct 11; bapt. Nov 30, 1800. Spon: Joh. Dieterich and wife, Barbara.

MIDDLETOWN CHURCH

Johannes of Johanes Backenstoss and Magdalena, b. Jan 31, 1765; bapt. Mar 10, 1765. Sponsors: parents.

Johan Wilhelm of Wilhelm Mass and Margaretha, b. Feb 23, 1758; bapt. Mar 10, 1765. Sponsors: Christian Roth and Ursula, his wife.

Cathrina of Wilhelm Mass and Margaretha, b. Dec 4, 1761; bapt. Mar 10, 1765. Sponsors: Wilhelm Mass.

Johan Peter of Wilhelm Mass and Margaretha, b. May 16, 1763; bapt. Mar 10, 1765. Sponsors: Peter Woulds and Lucia Erlissin.

Carolus of John De France and Elizabeth, b. Mar 10, 1765; bapt. Mar 10, 1765. Sponsors: Peter Woulds and Elizabeth.

Deborah of Abraham Bonn and Rebecca, b. Feb 25, 1756; bapt. Feb 25, 1765. Sponsors: Peter Woulds and Elizabeth.

John of John Dunkan and Eleonorah, b. Feb 25, 1765; bapt. Feb 25, 1765. Sponsors: Parents.

Abraham of Jacob Walter and Juliana, b. May 26, 1765; bapt. Jun 16, 1765. Sponsors: Parents.

Johanes of Baltaser Lauber and Elizabeth, b. Sep 1, 1762; bapt. Aug 25, 1765. Sponsors: Adam Wagoner and Rosina Wagoner.

Johan Adam of Baltaser Lauber and Elizabeth, b. Sep 1, 1764; bapt. Jul 14, 1765. Sponsors: Adam Wagoner and Rosina, his wife.

Ludwig of Conrad Wolffly and Cathrina, b. Mar 2, 1766; bapt. Mar 19, 1766. Sponsors: Philip Barthomer and Eva, his wife.

Johan Godfried of Jacob Rudiseller and Barbara, b. Dec 21, 1765; bapt. Mar 19, 1766. Sponsors: J. Godfried Kretschman and Sophia, his wife.

Cathrina of Johanes Bossart and Cathrina, b. Oct 28, 1765, bapt. Mar 30, 1766. Sponsors: Georg Frey and Cathrina, his wife.

Johan Philip of Wilhelm Mass and Margreth, b. Jun 3, 1766; bapt. Oct 17, 1766. Sponsors: Joh. Phil. Bodamer. and Anna Eva, his wife.

Rebecca of John De France and Elizabeth, b. Nov 3, 1766, bapt. Dec 14, 1766. Sponsors: Peter Wulds and Elizabeth, his wife.

Friderich of John Backenstoss and Magdalena, b. Jan 2, 1767, bapt. Jan 11, 1767. Sponsors: Parents.

Johan Jacob of Philip Bodamer and Anna Eva, b. Dec 21, 1766; bapt. Jan 11, 1767. Sponsors: Conrad Wolffly and Cathrina, his wife.

Margreth of John Dunckah and Eleonora, b. Nov 2, 1766, bapt. Feb 8, 1767. Sponsors: Parents.

William of John Wall and Mary, b. Apr 18, 1767, bapt. Jul 13, 1767. Sponsors: Peter Wultz, Jr. and Nancy Wultz and Sorer Petri.

Joh. Philip of Philip Krafft and Ana Maria, b. Nov 23, 1767; bapt. Dec 14, 1767. Sponsors: Antoni Keller and Barbara, his wife.

Maria Dorothee of Jacob Graff and Eva, b. Nov 6, 1767; bapt. Dec 15, 1767. Sponsors: Jacob Jistler and Christina, his wife.

Cathrina of Christian Spath and Christina, b. Feb 7, 1768; bapt. Mar 6, 1768. Sponsors: Georg Frey and Cathrina, his wife.

Margretha of Johanes Bossart and Cathrina, b. Dec 21, 1767; bapt. Mar 6, 1768. Sponsors: Heinrich Schaffer and Anna Ferena, his wife.

Anna Maria of Conrad Wolffly and Cathrina, b. Apr 17, ----; bapt. Mar 6, 1768. Sponsors: Georg Philip Jaquin and Cathrina, his wife.

Anna Maria of Joh. Jacob Burkhard and Anna, b. Jun, 1763; bapt. May 31, 1768. Sponsors: Jacob Kistler and Christina, his wife.

Joh. Jacob of Joh. Jacob Burkhard and Anna, b. Sep 14, 1765; bapt. May 31, 1768. Sponsors: *Eodem testes.*

Margreth of Joh. Jacob Burkhard and Anna, b. Feb 15, 1768, bapt. May 31, 1768. Sponsor: Barbarah LaRue.

Eva of Melchior Stahelin and Cathrina, b. Apr 11, 1768; bapt. May 31, 1768. Sponsors: Jacob Groff and Eva, his wife.

Jane of Edward Bez and Sarah, b. Jan 14, 1768; bapt. May 31, 1768. Sponsors: Melchoir Stahelin and Cathrina, his wife.

Mary Dorothea of Jacob Lochman and Barbarah, b. Jul 7, 1768; bapt. Jul 25, 1768. Sponsors: Parents.

John Christian of Leong Eshenauer and Margreth, b. ----; bapt. Jul 25, 1758 Sponsor: Christian Alleman.

Eliz. of Willm. Wall and Elizabeth, b. Jul 13, 1768; bapt. Jul 25, 1768. Sponsors: James Catch and Sussannah, his wife.

Maria Elizabetha of Adam Meyer and Anna Maria, b. Jul 22, 1768; bapt. Aug 20, 1768. Sponsors: Henry Schaffer and Anna Ferena, his wife.

Dina of Thomas Brown and Mary, b. Jun 6, 1768, bapt. Aug 21, 1768. Sponsors: James Ketch and Sussannah, his wife.

Mary Elizabeth of Johan Bodamer and Cathrina, b. Sep 13, 1768; bapt. Oct 16, 1768. Sponsors: Christoph Shap. and Margretha, his wife.

Anna Maria of John Mezgar and Anna Maria, b. Sep 12, 1768; bapt. Oct 16, 1768. Sponsor: Barbara La Rue.

Johanes of Jacob Kistler and Christina, b. Aug 23, 1768; bapt. Oct 19,

1768. Sponsors: Jacob Graff and Eva, his wife.

Anna Maria of Saml. Ziriacy and Elizabeth, b. Oct 25, 1768, bapt. Jan 16, 1769. Sponsors: Philip Krafft and Anna Maria, his wife.

Cathrina of Michael Fischer and Anna Maria, b. Oct 2, 1768, bapt. Jan 16, 1769. Sponsors: Georg Gross and Cathrina, his wife.

FREDERICKTOWN CHURCH (HUMMELSTOWN)

Melchoir of Melchoir Ram and Rebecca, b. Feb 15, 1762; bapt. Apr 14, 1765. Sponsors: Parents.

Eva Christina of Christoph Reichwein and Dorothea, b. Aug 25, 1765; bapt. Sep 25, 1765. Sponsor: Anna Eva Brouchin.

Fredrick of John Folk and Elizabeth Wolff, b. Jul 8, 1765, bapt. Oct 20, 1765. Sponsors: Peter Wolff and Hanah, his wife.

Ann Barbara of Martin Stahelin and Mary Margreth, b. Aug 27, 1765; bapt. Dec 15, 1765. Sponsors: Godfried Campher and Mary Magd. Lambertin.

Johanes of Melchoir Ram and Rebecca, b. Sep 22, 1765; bapt. Dec 15, 1765. Sponsors: John Brundle and Cathrina.

Johan Melchoir of John Brundle and Cathrina, b. Feb 16 1766; bapt. Feb 17, 1766. Sponsors: Melchoir Ram and Rebecca, his wife.

Johan Frederick of Balthaser Lauber and Elizabeth, b. Feb 17, 1766; bapt. Mar 9, 1766. Sponsors: Fridrich Bandstetter and Anna Barbara, his wife.

Rebecca of Michael Hook and Margreth, b. Feb 17, 1766; bapt. Mar 31, 1766. Sponsors: Melchoir Ram and Rebecca, his wife.

Sussannah of Charles Wetherhold and Sussannah, b. Oct 7, 1766; bapt. Oct 19, 1766. Sponsors: Sussannah, mater filia.

Jonas of Peter Schweyger and Anna Christina, b. Feb 25, 1767; bapt. Mar 10, 1767. Sponsors: Jonas Voght and Eva, his wife.

Joh. Jacob of Andr. Killinger and Anna, b. Feb 20, 1767; bapt. Mar 10, 1767. Sponsors: Peter Wolff and Hanah, his wife.

Sus. Margretha of Christoph Reichwein and Dorothea, b. Dec 5, 1766; bapt. Mar 10, 1767. Sponsors: Felton Brouch and Susannah Marg., his wife.

Johannes of Lorenz Brundle and Ferena, b. Mar 27, 1767; bapt. Apr 5, 1767. Sponsors: John Brundle and Cathrina.

Elizabeth of Jacob Burmann and Anna Maria, b. Feb 27, 1767; bapt. Apr 5, 1767. Sponsors: Daniel Burmann and Elizabeth Werner.

Sussannah of Antony Eller and Anna Cathrina, b. Feb 5, 1767; bapt. May 4, 1767. Sponsors: Philip Armbruster and Christina, his wife.

Joh. Georg of Georg Held and Magdalena, b. Jun 1, 1767; bapt. Jun 29, 1767. Sponsors: Lorenz Striker and Barbara, his wife.

John of Thomas McGahon and Mary, b. Jan 23, 1767; bapt. Jul 26, 1767. Sponsors: Philip Armbruster and Christina, his wife.

Magdalena of Georg. Obermeyer and Barbara, b. Aug 2, 1767; bapt. Aug 24, 1767. Sponsors: Heinrich Miller and Magdalena, his wife.

Cathrina of Lorenz Stricker and Barbara, b. Sep 5, 1767; bapt. Sep 20, 1767. Sponsors: Jacob Stricker and Magdalena Heldin.

Antony of Andreas Herauff and Maria Elizabetha, b. Feb 2, 1768, bapt. Apr 4, 1768. Sponsors: Joh. Antony Emrick and Margaretha, his wife.

Johann Heinrich of Balthazer Lauber and Elizabeth, b. Feb 16, 1768; bapt. Mar 6, 1768. Sponsors: Jacob Krieger and Elizabeth, his wife.

Johannes of Patrick Moor and Margretha, b. Feb 22, 1768; bapt. Mar. 6, 1768. Sponsors: Georg Obermeyer and Barbara, his wife.

Georg Michael of Michael Schaffer and Christina Barbara, b. Apr 7, 1768; bapt. May 1, 1768. Sponsors: Fridrich Forster and Gretha Barbara, his wife.

Rosina Cathrina of Pfanenkuchen and Cathrina, b. Apr 1, 1768; bapt. May 1, 1768. Sponsors: Fridrich Humel and Rosina, his wife.

John Jacob of Jacob Burman and Maria, b. Apr 10, 1768; bapt. May 1, 1768. Sponsors: Jacob Werner and Barbara, his wife.

Cathrina of Michael Hook and Margreth, b. ----; bapt. May 1, 1768. Sponsors: Adam Greiner and Cathrina, his wife.

Cathr. Elizabeth of Philip Fisher and Cathrina Margretha, b. May 31, 1768; bapt. Jul 25, 1768. Sponsors: John Wunderlich and Eliz. his wife.

Cathrina of Melchoir Ram and Rebecca, b. Jul 20, 1768; bapt. Aug 21, 1768. Sponsors: John Brundle and Cathrina, his wife.

Cathrina of John Brundle and Cathrina, b. Aug 4, 1768; bapt. Aug 21, 1768. Sponsors: Melchoir Ram and Rebecca, his wife.

Cathr. Elizab. of George Ezweyler and Maria, b. Feb 15, 1768; bapt. Aug 21, 1768. Sponsors: Jacob Albrecht and child's mother.

Jacob of Abraham Stahelin and Barbara, b. Aug 17, 1768; bapt. Aug 21, 1768. Sponsors: Jacoh Kettering and Rebeccah Guntherin.

HOFFMAN REFORMED CHURCH

Baptisms by unknown

Anna Maria of Johannes Reuter and Anna Maria, b. Sep 13, 1785.
Spon: Baltzar Ramberg and Anna Maria.
Johannes of Sebastian Steinbrecher and Susanna, b. Sep 28, 1785.
Spon: Adam Weiss and Margareta.
Daniel of Johanna Nicklas Hoffman and Margareta, b. Oct 9, 1785.
Spon: Christian Hofman.
Susanna of Peter Wiljer and Magdalena, b. Nov 18, 1781. Spon: ---
König.
Adam and Eva, twins of Peter Wiljer and Magdalena, b. Sep 10, 1785.
Spon: Henrich Höhn and Sarah, Georg Deibler and Elis.
Maria Elisabetha of Andreas Riegel and Catharina, b. Dec 23, 1785.
Spon: Peter Hofman and Maria Sarah.
Anna Margareta of Jacob Herman and Margaretha, b. Mar 9, 1786.
Spon: Henrich Höhn and Maria Sarah.
Elisabetha of Johannes Hofmann and Anna Maria, b. Jul 12, 1781.
Spon: Barbara Hofmann.
Christina Magdalena of Jacob Schott and Margareta, b. Oct 3, 1781.
Spon: Adam Kuber and Christina.
Georg Daniel of Henrich Witmer and Catharina, b. Sep 30, 1781.
Spon: Georg Reiter and wife.
Anna Catharina of Philip Knutzelman and Anna Catharina, b. May
12, 1781. Spon: Henrich Schreckengast and Catharina.
Catharina of Jonas McLien and Magdalena, b. Aug 18, 1781. Spon:
Johannes Reuter and Anna Maria.
Maria Sarah of Martin Neubäcker and Anna Margaretha, b. Jun 24,
1782. Spon: Peter Hofman and Sarah.
Catharina Elisabetha of Georg Müng? and Barbara, b. May 11, 1782.
Spon: Friedrich Paul and Catharina.
Johann Philip of Jacob Herrman and Margareta, b. Sep 22, 1782.
Spon: Ludwig Schott, Sr. and Barbara.
Elisabetha of Georg Bofington and Barbara, b. Dec 23, 1782. Spon:
Johannickel Hofman and Margaretha.
Johann Adam of Henrich Höhn and Sarah, b. Jan 17, 1783. Spon:
Johannes Hofman and Anna Maria.
Catharina of Johannes Hofman and Anna Maria, b. Jan 16, 1784.
Spon: Henrich Höhn and Maria Sarah.

Catharina of Ludwig Schütz and Elisabetha, b. Mar 7, 1784. Spon: Johann Kobus Hofman and Anna Margaretha.

Andreas of Henrich Wolf and Eva, b. Feb 10, 1784. Spon: Johann Kobus Hofman and Anna Margaretha.

Johannes of Baltzer Ramberger and Anna Maria, b. Nov 29, 1783. Spon: Johann Hofman and Anna Margaretha.

Maria of Michael Gälly and Anna Catharina, b. May 2, 1783. Spon: Jacob Herman and Anna Margaretha.

James of James McLein and Magdalena, b. Sep 16, 1783. Spon: Jacob Hofman and Catharina.

Samuel of Philip Rauschkolb and Anna Maria, b. May 26, 1784. Spon: Peter Hofman and Maria Sarah.

Hannah of Peter Schmitt and Anna Maria, b. Jan 21, 1784. Spon: Hannah Colmann.

Isaac of Georg Bofington and Barbara, b. Aug 8, 1784. Spon: Peter Hofman and Maria Sarah.

Johannes of Christian Stutzman and Elisabeth, b. Nov 16, 1784. Spon: Johannes Herman and Anna.

Anna Elisabetha of Georg Deibler and Elisabetha, b. Nov 26, 1784. Spon: Matheis Deibler and Anna Catharina.

Simon of Johannes Sallate and Margretha, b. Mar 12, 1785. Spon: Jacob Hofman and Catharina.

Peter of Johann Werner and Margretha, b. Sep 4, 1785. Spon: John Hofman and Anna Maria.

Ludwig of Jacob Schott and Margretha, b. Sep 3, 1785. Spon: Ludwig Schott, Jr. and Catharina.

Elisabetha of Adam Lasch and Susanna, b. Sep 17, 1785. Spon: Elisabetha Lasch.

Baptisms by Anthony Hautz, 1791-1797

Johann Nicolaus of Johann Nicolaus Hofman and Anna Margaretha, b. Nov 25, 1790. Spon: Henrich Werf(?) and Christina.

Catharina of Wilhelm Bordner and Elisabetha, b. Apr 15, 1791. Spon: Johannes Hofman and Anna Maria.

Johannes of Ludwig Schitz and Elisabetha, b. Mar 13, 1791. Spon: Joh. Nocolaus Hofman and Anna Margaretha.

Catharina of Jonathan Miller and Anna Maria, b. Dec 9, 1790. Spon: Jacob Woland and Maria Magdalena.

Rosina of Friedrich Stein and Abalonia, b. Feb 8, 1791. Spon: Rosina Lamm, single.

Magdalena of Henrich Wolf and Eva, b. Oct 7, 1790. Spon: Peter Wingert and Magdalena.

Jacoby of Jacoby Assman and Maria Greth, b. May 11, 1791. Spon: Parents.

Jacob of Henrich Henn and Maria, b. Jun 22, 1789. Spon: Parents.

Samuel Tobias of Johan Friedrich Dupendorf and Anna, b. Jan 21, 1791, bapt. --- 12, 1791. Spon: Johannes Schiesly and Catharina.

Magdalena of Johannes Hoffman and Anna Maria, b. Jul 16, 1791. Spon: Catharina Herrman.

Johannes of Johannes Hänn and Margareth, b. May 15, 1791. Spon: Johannes Hoffman and Anna Maria.

Johann Henrich of Peter Schock and Gretha (Margareth), b. Oct 26, 1789. Spon: Rudolf Peter and Clara.

Johannes of Nicolaus Bahner and Margretha, b. Sep 7, 1791. Spon: Conrath Dietz and Margretha.

Johann Martin of Martinus Neubeck and Margaretha, b. Mar 11, 1791. Spon: Christian Hoffman and Susanna.

Ann of Johannes Stahlman and Rebecca, b. Jun 25, 1789. Spon: Johann Nicolaus Hoffman and Anna Margreth.

Johannes of Johannes Tschop and Barbara, b. Mar 3, 1792. Spon: Feliz Tschop and Maria.

Daniel of Jonathan Miller and Anna Maria, b. May 3, 1792. Spon: Johannes Wohland.

Susanna of Johannes Bordner and Susanna, b. Mar 26, 1792. Spon: Mathaeus Däubler.

Rahel of Georg Boffington and Barbara, b. Apr 3, 1792. Spon: Johannes Hoffman and Anna Maria.

Susanna Catharina of Johannes Stahlman and Rebecca, b. Jan 1, 1792. Spon: Christian Hoffman and Susanna.

Catharina of Johannes Belles and Catharine, b. Jun 6, 1796. Spon: Peter Belles and Catharina.

Margreth of Daniel Salladee and Maria, b. Jun 7, 1796. Spon: Margreth Salladee.

Anna Maria of Adam Ramberger and Anna Maria, b. Aug 15, 1796. Spon: Michael Martin and Anna Maria.

Christina of Jonathan Miller and Anna Maria, b. Sep 18, 1796. Spon: Michael Sallade and Christina.

Magdalena of Peter Willo and Anna Maria, b. Aug 4, 1796. Spon:

Peter Wiljer and Magdalena.

Susanna of Johannes Bordner and Susanna, b. Oct 2, 1796. Spon: Henrich Höhn and Sarah.

Johannes of Jacob Huber and Catharina, b. Sep 25, 1796. Spon: Hardman Rickert and Magdalena.

Susanna of Henrich Wolf and Eva, b. Sep 19, 1796. Spon: Michael Sallade and Christina.

Barbara of Georg Zeller and Margaretha, b. Mar 3, 1796. Spon: Johannes Bosshaar and Catharina.

Bernart of --- Schreiner and Elisabeth, b. Oct 20, 1790. Spon: Johannes Hofman and Christina.

(This and the following baptisms are not by Hautz)

Wilhelm of Wilhelm Jung and Elisabetha, b. Jun 18, 1791. Spon: Elisabeth Späth.

Peter and Daniel of Georg Michael Hag and Catharina, b. Dec 13, 1796. Spon: Peter Wilgert, Catharina Boshart, Mathais Hag and Susanna.

John of Mathais Grünewalt and Maria, b. Mar 6, 1797. Spon: John Hofman and Maria.

John of Georg Herman and Catharina, b. Feb 20, 1797. Spon: Michael Salatin and Christina.

Benjamin of Levy Buffington and Susanna, b. Dec 30, 1796. Spon: Nicholas Hoffman and Margaretha.

Anna Maria of Johannes Deibler and Margretha, b. Feb 9, 1797. Spon: Johannes Hofman and Anna Maria.

Andreas of Andreas Daniel and Susanna, b. Jan 24, 1797. Spon: Andreas Ritzman and Anna Margaretha. (Entered by A. Hautz)

Sarah of Henrich Schafstall and Elisabetha, b. Oct 14, 1792. Spon: Nicolaus Hofman and Margretha.

Johannes of Christian Hoffman and Susanna, b. Sep 17, 1973. Spon: Johannes Riegel and Cath. Neubecker.

(This and the next six entries by A. Hautz)

Johaann Philip of Wilhelm Bordner and Elisabeth, b. Aug 12, 1793. Spon: Philip Haack and Elisabeth Etzweiler.

Christian of Jacob Huber and Catharina, b. Aug 24, 1793. Spon: Chirstian Hoffman and Susanna.

Sarah of Johann Nicolaus Hoffman and Margreth, b. Feb 4, 1793. Spon: Henrich Hähn and Sarah.

Elisabeth of Ludwig Schitz and Elisabeth, b. Jul 22, 1793. Spon: Susanna Hoffman.

Susanna of Peter Schaafstall and Catharina, b. Feb 28, 1793. Spon: Nicolaus Hoffman and Margreth.

Magdalena of Andreas Riegel and Catharina, b. Jun 24, 1793. Spon: Georg Bofington and Barbara.

Johannes of Johannes Bortner and Susanna, b. Aug 10, ---, bapt. Oct 19, (1793). Spon: Johannes Hoffman.

Joh. Jacob of Peter Weber and Catharina, b. Oct 15, ---, bapt. Nov 28, 1794. Spon: Matheis Teubler and Catharina.

Johannes of Johannes Billes and Catharina, b. Apr 6, 1795. Spon: Rudolph Peter and Clara.

Catharina of Peter Schaffstall and Catharina, b. Apr 15, ---. Spon: Levi Bofington and Susanna.

Solomon of Levi Boffington and Susanna, b. Jan 29, ---. Spon: Nicklaus Hoffman and Margaretha.

Johannes of Nicklaus Hoffman and Margretha, b. Dec 9, (179)4. Spon: Johannes Hoffman and Anna Maria.

Susanna of Joh. Hoffman, Jr. and Christina, b. Apr 19, 1795. Spon: Christian Hoffman and Susanna.

Johannes of Georg Michael Haag, b. Mar ---. Spon: Johannes Hoffman and Christina.

Johann Jacob of Jacob Dieter and A. Magdalena, b. May --, 1975. Spon: Friedrich Leobolt.

Eva Margretha of Adam Ramberger and Maria, b. ---, 10, 1795. Spon: Samuel Bayer and Eva Margretha.

Jeremias of Johannes Stahlman and Rebecca, b. Mar 17, ----. Spon: Nicolaus Hoffman and Anna Margreth.

Johannes of Adam Bahr and Susanna, b. Oct 28, ----. Spon: Andreas Daniel and Susanna.

Maria Catharina of Henrich Witmer and Cathrina, b. Sep 23, 1794. Spon: Anna Maria Hähn.

Georg of Georg Boffenden and wife, b. --- 12, ---. Spon: Johannes Hoffman.

Anna Maria of Ludwig Schitz and Elisabeth, b. Aug 17, 1795. Spon: Peter Schaffstall and Catharina.

Peter of Adam Wolf and Christina, b. Jun 21, 1795. Spon; Peter Wilgert and Charlotta Deibler.

Philip of Peter Bordner and Cathrina, b. Apr 16, 1796. Spon: Philip Korden and Dorothea.

Henrich of Henrich Heuer and Catharina, b. Apr 15, 1796. Spon: Peter Hen.

Peter of Henrich Ramberger and Elisabeth, b. Nov 12, 1795. Spon: Peter Ritzman and Catharina.

Anna Maria of Georg Minch and Anna Barbara, b. Jan 29, 1796. Spon; Joseph Paul and Anna Maria.

Johannes of Bernard Umholtz and Catharina, b. Jan 18, 1796. Spon: Georg Herman.

Anna Maria of Matheis Däubler and Anna Catharina, b. Mar 12, 1796. Spon: William Bordner and Elisabeth.

J. Jacob of Adam Kuper and A. Christina, b. ---, 9, 1975. Spon: Jacob Schott and Anna Margareth.

Jacob of Jacob Lautenschläger and Sophia, b. Mar 6, 1796. Spon; Jacob Sallade and Susanna.

Jacob of Johannes Umholtz and Catharina Hoffman, b. Feb 17, 1796. Spon: Jacob Lautenschläger and Sophia.

Johannes of Georg Holtzman and Elisabeth, b. Mar 21, 1796. Spon: Joh. Hoffman and Anna Maria.

Catharina of Andreas Daniel and Susanna, b. Dec 10, 1795. Spon: Adam Bahr and Susanna.

Joh. Jacob of Peter Forne and Catharina, b. May 20, 1796. Spon; Christian Hoffman and Susanna.

Rebecca of Joseph Staalman and Nellena, b. Jun 2, 1796. Spon; Andreas Riegel and Catharina.

Joh. Philip of Johannes Marter and Elisabetha, b. Apr 27, 1796. Spon: Jacob Schott and Anna Margareth.

Georg Daniel of Christian Hoffman and Susanna, b. Jul 1, 1796. Spon: Georg Boffenton and Barbara.

Anna Catharina of Johannes Tschop and Barbara, b. Jul 1, 1796. Spon; Casper Hechart and Anna Catharina.

Johannes of Henrich Schafstall and Elisabeth, b. Sep 10, 1796. Spon: Christian Hofman and Susanna.

Susanna Catharina of Georg Bofington and Barbara, b. Feb 15, 1797. Spon: Christian Hofman and Susanna.

Jacob of Philp Hock and Charlotta, b. Nov 1, 1790. Spon: John Bosshart.

Catharina of Philip Hock and Charlotta, b. Sep 4, 1792. Spon: Catharina Bosshart.

Elisabetha of Philip Hock and Charlotta, b. Aug 11, 1794. Spon: Catharina Elisabeth Bosshart.

Christian of Philip Hock and Charlotta, b. Mar 19, 1796. Spon: Michael Salate and Christina.

Sarah of Johannes Hänn and Margreth, b. Sep 5, 1796. Spon: Christian Hofman, Jr. and Susanna.

Johan Christian of Henrich Ramberger and Elisabeth, b. Jul --, 1797. Spon: Christian Hoffman and Susanna.

Anna Magdalena of Valentin Sommerlad and Anna Elisabeth, b. Jul 18, 1797. Spon: Elisabeth Späth.

Johannes of Jacob Miller and Sarah, b. May ---, 1797. Spon: Henrich Ramberger and Elisabeth.

Johannes of Johannes Herrman and A. Maria, b. Aug 23, 1797. Spon: Isaac Heller and Catharina.

Susanna of Adam Ramberger and Anna Maria, b. Sep 2, 1797. Spon: Margaretha Werner.

Catharina of Henrich Heyen and Catharina, b. Jul 26, 1798. Spon: Christian Hoffman and Susanna.

Barbara of Wilhelm Bortner and Elisabeth, b. Oct 27, 1797. Spon: Johannes Hofman, Jr. and Christina.

Georg of Johannes Warner, Jr. and Anna Maria, b. Nov 25, 1797. Spon: Johannes Warner, Sr., and Margretha.

Johannes of Johannes Umholtz and Catharina, b. Feb 20, 1798. Spon: Johannes Hofman and Anna Maria.

Susanna of Johannes Umholt and Catharina, b. Mar 9, 1796. Spon: Jacob Herrman and Margretha.

Elisabetha of Christian Schnug and Elisabetha, b. Dec 28, 1797. Spon: Michael Salate and Christina.

Harman of Philip Hock and Charlotta, b. Jan 30, 1798. Spon: Harman Rückert and Magdalena.

Jacob of Gottfried Schneider and Catharina, b. Sep 9, 1797; bapt. Apr 29, (1798). Spon: Jacob Schneider and Catharina.

Adam of Adam Bär and Susanna, b. Feb 5, 1798; bapt. Apr 29, ----. Spon: Peter Wild and Maria Magdalena.

Johann Georg of Nicolaus Hofman and Anna Marg., b. Mar 13, 1798; bapt. Apr 29, ----. Spon: Georg Puffentaun and Barbara.

Catharina of Peter Portner and Catharina, b. Apr 27, 1798; bapt. Apr 29, ---. Spon: Wilhelm Portner and Elisabeth.

Magdalena of Peter Schafstall and Cath., b. Oct 27, 1797; bapt. Apr 29, 1798. Spon: Christian Hofman and Susanna.

Peter of Christian Hofman and Susanna, b. Mar 17, 1798; bapt. Apr 29, 1798. Spon: Peter Schafstall and Catharina.

Elisabeth of Adam Wolf and Christina, b. Jan 5, 1798; bapt. Apr 29, 1798. Spon: Adam Bär and Susanna.

Magdalena of Georg Bechtel and Anna Maria, b. Nov 19, 1797; bapt. Apr 29, 1798. Spon: Matthias Weimer and Magdalena.

Anna Maria of Peter Weber and Catharina, b. Apr 1, 1798; bapt. Apr 29, 1798. Spon: Johannes Hofman and Anna Maria.

Sarah of Jonathan McCruny and Maria, b. Feb 24, 1797. Spon: Nicolaus Hoffman and Margaretha.

Johannes of Michael Schädel, Jr. and Maria, b. Apr 15, 1798. Spon: Adam Weiss and Margaretha.

Jacob of Jacob Salade and Susanna, b. May 19, (1798); bapt. Jul 29, --. Spon: Peter Ritzmann and Cath. Elisabeth.

Magdalena of Jonathan Müller and Anna Maria, b. May 6, (1798); bapt. Jul 29, ---. Spon: Andreas Riegel and Catharina.

Sarah of Johannes Haen and Margaretha, b. Sep 5, 1796. Spon: Christian Hofman and Susanna.

Maria Elisabetha of Jonathan McCruny and Maria, b. Mar 24, 1791. Spon: Sarah Dietrich.

Anna Magdalena of Jonathan McCruny and Maria, b. Mar 17, 1793. Spon: Magdalena Rücker.

Samuel of Jonathan McCruny and Maria, b. May 8, 1795. Spon: Christian Hofman and Susanna.

Christophel of Johannes Jäger and Catharina, b. Sep 8, 1798. Spon: Stoffel Jäger.

Maria Catharina of Jonathan McCrury and Maria, b. Oct 19, 1798. Spon: Joh. Hoffman and Anna Maria.

Magdalena of Joh. Bälles and Catharina, b. Aug 28, 1798. Spon: Johan Philip Hamman and Maria Margretha.

Margaretha Magdalena of John Tschopp and Barbara, b. Feb 22, 1798. Spon: Johannes Warner and Margaretha.

Christina of Mathaeus Deubler and Catharina, b. Oct 21, 1798. Spon: Johannes Hoffman, Jr. and Christina.

Johannes of Jonathan McCrury and Polly, b. Apr 12, ---; bapt. Jul 7, 1799. Spon: Johannes Hofmann and Christina.

Susanna of Levi Puffenton and Susanna, b. Nov 7, 1798; bapt. Jul 7, ---. Spon: Geo. Puffenton and Barbara.

Margaretha of George Puffentaun and Barbara, b. Aug 22, 1799; bapt. Sep 29, 1799. Spon: Marg. Hofmann.

Elisabeth of Michael Schedel and Catharina, b. Aug 17, 1799; bapt. Sep 29, 1799. Spon: Georg Gundelein and Catharina.

Johannes of Daniel Deibler and A. Maria, b. Jan 4, 1799; bapt. Sep 29, 1799. Spon: Johannes Hoffman and Christina.

Christian of Christian Hoffman and Susanna, b. Jul 30, 1799; bapt.
Sep 3, 1799. Spon: Nicolaus Hoffman and Margretha.

Joh. Peter of Peter Willo and Maria Salome, b. Feb 22, 1799; bapt.
Sep 3, 1799. Spon: Johannes Messler and Catharina.

Michael of Wilhelm Bordner and Elisabetha, b. Sep 29, 1799; bapt.
Nov 10, 1799. Spon: Michael Koppenhöffer and Catharina.

Susanna of Johannes Herman and Elisabeth, b. Nov 6, 1799. Spon:
Johannes Hoffman and Christina.

Elisabetha of Jacob Miller and Sarah, b. Oct 7, 1799. Spon: Henrich
Ramberger and Elisabth.

Elisabetha of Johannes Hoffman, Jr. and Christina, b. ----. Spon:
Elisabetha Hofman.

Daniel of Johannes Hofman, Jr. and Christina, b. Feb 19, 1800. Spon:
Johannes Hofman and Anna Maria.

Elisabetha of Friedrich Lubolt and Elisabetha, b. Jan 9, 1800. Spon:
Catharina Neyen.

Elisabeth Lubolt of Friedrich Lubolt and Elisabeth, d. Mar 8, 1814
age 17 yrs 2 mos.

Samuel of Leonard Schneider and Anna Maria, b. Nov 10, 1799; bapt.
Jan 16, 1800. Spon: Christian Schott.

Cathrina of Friedrich Stein and Abolonia, b. Dec 22, 1799. Spon:
Friedrich Stein and Abolonia.

Simon of Peter Schafstall and Catharine, b. Mar 1, 1800; bapt. Jan
16, ----. Spon: Johannes Hofman and Elisabeth.

Elisabetha of Adam Ramberger and Anna Maria, b. May 2, 1800.
Spon: George Matter and Catharina.

Elisabetha of Johannes Bordner and Susanna, b. Aug 28, 1800. Spon:
Wilhelm Bordner and Elisabetha.

Anna Maria of Peter Wiljer, Jr. and Catharina, b. Sep 21, 1800. Spon:
Philip Wiljer and Ann Margretha Hoffman.

Barbara of Johannes Hofman and Anna Maria, b. Dec 23, 1800. Spon:
Leonhart Sneider and Anna Maria.

Catharina of Johannes Herman and Elisabetha, b. Nov 16, 1800.
Spon: Johannes Hoffman and Anna Maria.

Barbara of Mathias Haag and Susanna, b. Nov 28, 1800. Johannes
Deubler and Margaretha.

Catharina of Henrich Ramberger and Elisabetha, b. Oct 3, 1800.
Spon: Jacob Huber and Catharina.

Barbara of Wilhelm Bordner and Elisabetha, b. Oct 27, 1800. Spon:
Johannes Hoffman and Christina.

Georg of Johannes Werner, Jr. and Anna Maria, b. Nov 25, 1797.
Spon: Johannes Werener and Margaretha.
Cathrina of Friedrich Stein and Abolonia, b. Dec 22, 1799. Spon:
Friedrich Stein and Abolonia.
Wilhelm of George Zeller and Margretha, b. Mar 18, 1800. Spon:
Jacob Huber and Catharina Elisabeth.

CATHECHUMENS AND COMMUNICANTS.
performed by Mr. Hautz Jul 18, 1791

Jacob Trautman
Abraham Trautman
Peter Höhn
Georg Höhn
Johannes Hoffman
Abraham Wilgert
Peter Wilgert
Christian Schott
Johannes Dieterich
Leonhart Umholz
Leonhart Schneider
Johannes Hänn
Johannes Werner
Georg Buffington
Ely Buffington
Levy Buffington
Josua Assman
Jacoby Assman
Peter Schafstal
Jacob Weber
Stophel Schneider
Jacob Hoock
Nicolaus Hoffman
Catharina Hoffman
Susanna Hoffman
Catharina Höhn
Magdalena Wilgert
Anna Maria Schott

Susanna Höhn
Catharina Hänn
Greth Hänn
Elisabetha Hänn
Sarah Hänn
Maria Werner
Elisabetha Jaeger
Margareth Dietz
Barbara Schiesli
Catharina Jaeger
Magdalena Weber
Catharina Wilt
Esther Wilt
Greth Etzweiler
Maria Ditty
Magdalena Kupper
Anna Maria Heller
Magdalena Riegel
Sarah Hoffman
Catharina Hoock
Magdalena Frantz
Catharina Bechtold

LYKENS VALLEY LOWER CHURCH

Baptisms Rev. John Wm. Hendel, Sr.

Valentin of Jacob Strikler and Dorothea, b. Mar 18, 1774; bapt. Jun 8, 1774. Spon: Valentin Brauch and wife, Susanna.

Maria Barbara of Georg Münich and Maria Margaretha, b. Feb 4, 1774; bapt. Jun 8, 1774. Spon: Ludwig Schott and wife Maria Barbara.

Margaretha of Jacob Weber and Anna Maria, b. Apr 17, 1774; bapt. Jun 8, 1774. Spon: Christoph Lerch and wife Anna Margaretha.

Isaak of Heinrich Wilhelm and Sarah, b. Aug 31, 1746; bapt. Aug 16, 1774. Spon: ---.

Joh. Friedrich of Johannes Kistler and Anna Maria, b. Jun 20, 1774, bap. Aug 17, 1774. Spon: Joh. Schiessley and wife Sarah.

Christina Catharina of Wilhelm Reutter and Catharina, b. Jul 29, 1774; bapt. Aug 17, 1774. Spon: Michael Salide and wife Christina.

Anna Maria of Johannes. Nikolaus Hoffman and Anna Margaretha, b. Feb 12, 1775; bapt. May 1, 1775. Spon: Johannes Hoffman and wife Anna Maria.

Johan Georg of Georg Siehl and Magdalena, b. Dec 24, 1774; bapt. May 1, 1774. Spon: Georg Nihl and wife Magdalena.

Anna Maria of Christoph Lang and Ursula, b. Jan 28, 1775; ba: May 1, 1775. Spon: Johannes Kistler and wife Dorothea.

Joh. Christian of Joh. Jacob Schott and Ann Margaretha, b. Nov 24, 1774; bapt. May 1, 1775. Spon: Ludwig Schott.

Elisabetha of Matheyss Döbler(?) and Barbara, b. Feb 11, 1775; ba: May 1, 1775. Spon: Anna Margaretha Stöberlin.

Johan Philip of Joh. Peter Ville and Magdalena, b. Apr 7, 1775; ba: May 1, 1775. Spon: Abraham Shorah and Margaretha Shorah.

Maria Catharina of David Tuben (Tubs) and Elisabeth, b. Feb 6, 1774; bapt. May 1, 1775. Spon: Heinrich Dubs and wife Catharina.

Johannes of Isaak Wilhelm and Elisabetha, b. Feb 12, 1775; bapt. May 1, 1775. Spon: Magdalena Brown.

Joseph of Simon Brand and Margaretha, b. Nov 29, 1774; bapt. May 1, 1775. Spon: Jost Stöberlin.

Anna Margaretha of Matheyss Jeger and Magdalena, b. Nov 29, 1774; bapt. May 1, 1775. Spon: Anna Margaretha Hoffman.

Isabella of Thomas Campleton and Mary, b. Sep 2, 1773, bapt. May 1, 1775. Spon: The mother.

(Baptisms by supplies 1776-1778)

Magdalena of Jacob Weber and Anna Maria, b. Oct 30, 1776; bapt. ---.
Spon: Georg Nagle and wife.
Elisabeth of Joseph Braun and wife, b. May 15, 1776; bapt. Jul 27,
1776. Spon: Vallentin Brauch and wife.
Catharina Elisabeth of Hannes Bosert and Catharina, b. Nov 20,
1775, ba: Jul 2, 1776. Spon: Wilhelm Reuter and wife.
Margaretha Dorothea of Michael Goeller and Margaret, b. Mar 14,
1776, bapt. Jul 2, 1776. Spon: Michael Salledy and wife.
Johannes of Johannes Hoffman and Anna Maria, b. Jun 11, 1776,
bapt. Jun 19, 1776. Spon: Nicolaus Hoffman.
Susanna Catharina of Nicolaus Hoffman and Margaretha, b. May 5,
1776; bapt. Jun 19, 1776. Spon: Catharina Steinbrecher.
Nicolaus of Lenhart Schinderlot and Catharine, b. Apr 14, 1776; bapt.
Jun 19, 1776. Spon: Nicolaus Hoffman and wife.
Samuel of Jacob Rippass and Anna, b. Apr 13, 1776; bapt. Jul 21,
1776. Spon: Samuel Schura and Magdalena Schenider.
Samuel of Hannes Kistler and Anna Maria, b. Oct 21, (1776); bapt.
Feb --, 1777. Spon: Velde Brauch.
Elisabetha of Jost Stieber and Anna Margaretha, b. Sep 3, 1777;
bapt. ---, 1777. Spon: Philip Rauschkolb.
Anna Maria Margaret of Stephan Bieg and Maria Margaretha, b. Sep
9, 1777; bapt. Sep 15, 1777. Spon: Adam König and Maria Marg.
Stieger, both single.
Johannes of Martin Neubecker and wife, b. Oct 8, 1777; bapt. Nov 6,
1777. Spon: Johannes Hoffman.
--- of Johannes Hoffman and Maria, b. Nov 15, 1777; bapt. 1779.
Spon: ---.
Philip Jacob of Johann Saladin and Margaretha, nee Eberhardt, b.
Dec 26, 1778; bapt. Jul 4, 1779. Spon: Michael Saladin and wife.
Margaretha of David Rosch and Catharina, nee Wagner, b. Jun 13,
1779; bapt. Jul 6, 1779. Spon: Adam König, Jr. and Margaretha
Klein.

(Baptims by Rev. Samuel Dubendorff 1779-82)

Johann Philip of Philip Rauschkolb and Maria Anna, nee Regi, b. Nov 14, 1778; bapt. Jun ---, (1779). Spon: Philip Klinger.

Johann Adam of Christian Schnug and Anna Christiana nee Beyer, b. ---, bapt. Jun 14, (1779). Spon: Parents.

Joseph of David Hermann and Elisabeth nee Hön, b. Sep 13, (1779); bapt. Oct 3, 1779. Spon: Jacob Hermann and wife Margaretha.

Christina of Heinrich Wurffel and Christina, nee Steinbrecher, b. Sep 13, (1779); bapt. Oct 3, 1779. Spon: Dietrich Steinbrecher and wife Catharina.

Anna Maria of Peter Schmidt and Anna Maria, nee Herter, b. Oct 2, 1779; bapt. Oct 7, 1779. Spon: Johannes Hoffman and wife Anna Maria.

Abraham of Samuel [F.] Joray and Hannah, b. Feb 12, 1780; bapt. Mar 1, 1780. Spon: Abraham [F.] Joray, Jr. and Anna Maria Bretz.

Cathatharina of Jacob Schüssle and wife, b. Dec 20, 1779; bapt. Mar 5, 1780. Spon: Adam König, Jr. and Catharina Schüssle.

Daughter of John Michael Henney, an Irishman, b. ---; bapt. Aug 7, (1780) by Rev. Hendel. Spon: Martin Weber and wife.

Adam of Heinrich Meyer and Anna, nee Buffentaun, b. May 17, 1781; bapt. Jun 3, 1781. Spon: Adam König, Jr. and Eva Elisabeth Stüberling, single.

Elisabeth of Peter Heckardt and Anna Maria, nee Hüner, b. Dec 10, 1779; bapt. Mar 27, 1780. Spon: Johan Heckardt and wife, Elisabeth, nee Fischer.

Maria Elisabeth of Casper Heckardt and Catharina, nee Steinbrecher, b. Dec ---, 1779; ba: Mar 27, 1780. Spon: Ludwig Schütz and wife Maria Elisabeth.

Sebastian of Leonard Kirchstetter and Christina, nee Lünckerton, b. Dec 28, 1779; bapt. Mar 27, 1780. Spon: Sebastian Kirchstetter.

Johannes of Heinrich Wittmer and Catharina, nee Lösch, b. Mar 10, 1780; bapt. Mar 27, 1780. Spon: Christoph Wittmer and wife Christina.

Joh. Dieterich of Jaob Schneider and Anna Maria, nee Steinbrecher, b. ---, bapt. Mar 27, 1780. Spon: Dieterich Steinbrecher and wife.

Wilhelm of Brand Fischer and Margaret nee Reiter, b. Nov 24, 1779; bapt. Mar 27, 1780. Spon: Wilhelm Reiter and Margaretha Wittmer, single.

Johan Leonhardt of Daniel Stüberling and Eva Maria nee Kistner, b.

Mar 1, 1782; bapt. Mar 10, 1782. Spon: Johan Leonhardt Stüberling, Jr. and Barbara Kistner.

Johann George of Jacob Weber and wife Anna Maria, b. Feb 27, 1782; bapt. May 29, 1782. Spon: Johan Georg Nägele and Eva Elisabeth Stüberling.

Matthias of Matthias Deibler and Maria Barbara, nee Spiegel, b. Apr 27, 1782; bapt. Jul 2, 1782. Spon: Parents Matthias and Maria Barbara Deibler.

(Baptisms by Unkown supply)

Georg of Georg Etzweiler and Elisabeth, b. Feb 19, 1796. Spon: George Etzweiler and wife Elisabeth.

Catharina of Val. Welcker and Susanna, b. Feb 22, 1796. Spon: Adam König and Salome.

Johannes of ---, b. Feb 22, 1796. Spon: Johannes Wirth and Annamary.

Baptisms by Rev. Anthony Hautz

Magdalena of Johanes Ditty and Anna Maria, b. Apr 16, 1796. Spon: Parents.

Michael of Michael Schott and Elisabetha, b. Mar 31, 1796. Spon: Ludwig Schott and Catharina.

Henrich of Henrich Meck and Susanna, b. Oct 5, 1797. Spon: Parents.

Joh. Georg of Joh. Jost Scheidt and Elisabeth, b. Jan 15, 1797. Spon: Michael Bauer and Veronica.

Johannes of Henrich Siel and Catharina, b. Mar 14, 1797. Spon: Edman Li (torn) and Cath.

Daniel of Adam Stieber and Eva Maria, b. Oct 9, 1797. Spon: Michael Klein and Barbara.

Johannes of Adam Kupper and Christina, b. Jun 30, 1797. Spon: Johannes Martin and Elisabeth.

Anna of Henrich Kissel and Anna, b. Jul 8, 1791. Spon: Parents.

Mary of Henrich Kissel and Anna, b. Sep 27, 1793. Spon: Parents.

Henry of Henrich Kissel and Anna, b. Dec 30, 1795. Spon: Parents.

Daniel of Leonhardt Stieber and Susanna, b. Jan 20, 1798. Spon: Daniel Stieber and Eva Maria.

Anna of Georg Münig, b. Apr 9, 1798. Spon: George Paul and Catharina.

Johannes of Georg Groh and Ann, b. Dec 4, 1797. Spon: Parents.

Elisabeth of Stoffel Jäger and Eva Catharina, b. --- 21, 1797. Spon: Georg Nägely and Hanna.

Johannes of Henrich Kissel and Anna, b. Apr 27, 1798. Spon: Johannes Franck and Susanna.[Rissel, but hand written changed to Kissel)

Elisabetha of Henrich Siegel and Catharina, b. May 24, 1798. Spon: Philip Stieber and Elisabeth.

Susan Catharina of Michael Schott and Elisabetha, b. Jun 29, 1798. Spon: Catharina Leicht.

Jacob of Valentin Welcker and Susanna, b. Aug 10, 1798. Spon: Jacob Lindner and Catharina.

Next two entries are by a trained, but unknown hand)

Jacob of Jacob Lindner and Catharina, b. Jun 18, 1799, bapt. Jul 8, 1799. Spon: Catharina Lindner, grandmother.

Jacob of Abraham Schora and Elisabeth, b. Apr 5, 1799, bapt. Jul 8, 1799. Spon: Samuel Schora and Johanna.

Johannes of Georg Scheif and Anna, b. Nov 7, 1800; bapt. --- 1801. Spon: Abraham Schora.

(Entries of 1801 and 1802 were made by same hand)

Johannes of Jacob Groo and Elisabeth, b. Oct 9, 1800. Spon: Abraham Schora and Elisabeth.

Georg of Georg Feith and Rahel, b. Nov 26, 1800. Spon: Georg Negele and Hanna.

Adam of Stephan Lesch and Maria Margaret, b. Sep 17, 1800. Spon: Dietrich Steinbrecher and Catharina.

Anna Maria of Andreas Asmann and Anna Margaretha, b. Aug 17, 1799. Spon: Parents.

Maria Magdalena of Johannes Lang and Salome, b. Jun 27, 1798. Spon: Catharina McLen.

DEATHS (Burials by Rev. Samuel Dubendorff)

Mrs. Anna Barbara Jaeger, nee Schuster, b. at Lachen in the district of Neustadt in the Palatinate, b. Feb 15, 1733, d. Jul 27, 1779.

Margaretha Bieg, dau of Stephanus Bieg, schoolteacher here, and of his wife, Margaretha Bieg, nee Wachs, b. Sep 9, 1777, d. Aug 11, 1779.

Magdalena, dau of Johan Dedie, b. Oct 23, 1772, d. Aug 26, 1779.

Maria Elisabeth, dau of Peter Heckart, resident on the Machatonky,

and wife, Maria, nee Hüner, b. Jan 18, 1778, d. Sep 5, 1779.
Georg Stöberlein, son of Justus Stöberlein and wife, Philippina
Margaretha, nee Le Crone, b. Oct 19, 1773, d. Sep 6, 1779.
Charlotte Schaetel, wife of Michael Schaetel, linnenweaver, d. Oct,
1779.
George Siegel, d. Mar 9, 1813. George Siegel, age 36 yrs, 1 mo, 9
days.
Abraham Landes, of Hallifax, b. Apr 4, 1768 in Richland twp, Bucks
County, m. (1) Catharina Kinsch; had 4 children; m. (2) Susanna
Rewald, had 2 children. bapt. Feb 15, 1825, d. Mar 1, 1825, age 56
yrs, 10 mos, 24 days.

CATHECHUMES AND COMMUNICANTS

Aug 16, 1774.

Leonard Stöberlein
Daniel Stöberlein
Abraham Shorah
Samuel Shorah
Anna Catharina Schott
Christina Margaretha Schott
Anna Margaretha Shorah
Catharina Shorah
Anna Maria Kupfer
Agnes Schneider
Magdalena Schneider

Jul 1, 1777

Friedrich Wilhelm Bieg
Adam König
Adam Schweigert
Adam Kupper
Wilhelm Klein
Magdalena Schott
Susanna Shora

Anna Maria Margaretha
Stieber
Maria Schott
Barbara Paul
Elisabetha Ginder
Maria Kahn
Margaretha Klein
Catharina Isch

Sep 23, 1780

Heinrich Wittmer, 21 yrs.
Christoph Wittmer, 19 yrs.
Philip König, 15 yrs.
Friedrich Klein, 14 yrs.
George Negeli, 16 yrs.
Christoph Jaeger, 17 yrs.
Eva Elisab. Stiberlinger, 15
yrs.
Maria Eva Wagner, 15 yrs.
Salome Jorai, 15 yrs.
Maria Marg. Wittmer, 16 yrs.
Catharina Fuchs, 16 yrs.
Anna Maria Fuchs, 14 yrs.
Susanna Braun, 19 yrs.

Aug 10, 1782

George Riem, 20 yrs.
Christian Riem, 17 yrs
Johann Jaeger, 16 yrs.
Andreas Schweickardt, 17 yrs.
Joseph Negel, 15 yrs.
Joh. George Reuter, 18 yrs.
Anna Margaretha Ulsh, wife of
Abraham Joria, Jr. 25 yrs.
Elisabeth Jaeger, 14 yrs.
Margaretha Schott, 15 yrs.
Cathar. Elisab. Etschweiler, 15
yrs.

Aug, 1783

Friedrich Heckardt
Felix Tschopp
Jacob Tschopp
Johannes Mercki
Magdalena Tschopp
Margaretha, nee Reiger,
married Fischer
Hannah Schneider
Catharina Schneider

PAXTANG AND DERRY CHURCHES

MARRIAGE RECORDS

1757, Feb 11,	Allen, Samuel and Rebecca Smith.
1772, Mar --,	Anderson, James and Margaret Chambers.
1788, Apr 22,	Anderson, James and Esther Thom.
1773, Oct 14,	Bell, John and Martha Gilchrist.
1774, Jun 24,	Bell, Samuel and Ann Berryhill.
1796, Jul 7,	Bittner, Mr. and Mrs. Charlotte King.
1784, Mar 2,	Boal, Robert and Mary Wilson.
1776, --- --,	Boyd, Joseph and Elizabeth Wallace.
1796, May 19,	Brice, Alexander and Peggy Kearsley.
1746, Nov 6,	Brown, James and Eleanor Mordah.
1769, Oct 19,	Brown, William and Sarah Semple.
1774, Oct 7,	Brunson, Barefoot and Agnes White.
1771, Sep 24,	Buck, Elijah and --- ---.
1785, Jan 3,	Buck, William and Margaret Elliott.
1783, Feb 27,	Caldwell, Matthew and Mary Pinkerton.
1786, Apr 11,	Calhoun, David and Eleanor King.
1748, Jun 16,	Carson, James and Mary Espy.
1769, Apr 27,	Cavet, James and --- ---.
1800, Mar 19,	Chambers, Benjamin and Grace Stewart.
1771, Dec 5,	Chambers, Maxwell and Elizabeth ---.
1780, Jan 13,	Chesney, John and --- ---.
1769, Dec 14,	Christy, William and --- ---.
1790, Oct 14,	Clark, Charles and Elizabeth Robinson.
1783, Aug 7,	Clark, John and Mary Smith.
1775, Apr 13,	Clark, William and --- ---.
1780, --- --,	Cook, William and Sarah Simpson.
1777, Mar 20,	Cowden, James and Mary Crouch.
1778, Jan 22,	Crain, George and --- ---.
1787, Nov 20,	Culbertson, John and Mary Augeer.
1775, Mar 7,	Curry, Daniel and --- ---.
1774, Apr 14,	Curry, William and Agnes Curry.
1799, Feb 10,	Dentzell, John, Esq. and Jean Gilchrist.
1780, Jul 13,	Dickey, James and --- ---.
1778, Jan 13,	Dickey, John and --- ---.
1772, Dec 1,	Dickey, William and --- ---.
1777, Dec 4,	Dixon, George and --- ---.

1788, Jun 7,	Dixon, Sankey and Anna Cochran.
1779, Dec 14,	Donaldson, James and --- ---.
1774, Jan 9,	Dugal, Mr. and Sarah Wilson.
1795, Apr 21,	Dugal, Mr. and Jenny Hilton.
1779, Oct 5,	Duncan, Andrew and --- ---.
1741, Aug 13,	Elder, Rev. John and Mary Baker.
1751, Nov 5,	Elder, Rev. John and Mary Simpson.
1788, Jan 18,	Elder, John, Jr. and Sarah Kennedy.
1773, Sep 16,	Elder, Joshua and --- ---.
1783, May 27,	Elder, Joshua and --- ---.
1795, Jun 4,	Elder, Michael and Nancy McKinney.
1769, Feb 7,	Elder, Robert and --- ---.
1799, Mar 23,	Elder, Thomas and Catharine Cox.
1744, Sep 16,	Findlay, John and Elizabeth Harris.
1781, Mar 6,	Fleming, John and Nancy Neill.
1798, Sep 25,	Forster, John and Mary Elder.
1773, Nov 1,	Forster, William and Margaret Ayres.
1784, Dec 14,	Foster, Robert and Esther Renick.
1777, Nov 4,	Foster, Thomas and Jane Young.
1771, Nov 5,	Fulton, Benjamin and --- ---.
1774, Jun 16,	Fulton, Grizel and --- Wilson.
1780, Jan 16,	Fulton, Joseph and --- ---.
1744, Jun 14,	Fulton, Richard and Isabella McChesney.
1771, Dec 12,	Galbraith, Benjamin and --- ---.
1771, Aug 22,	Gilchrist, John and --- ----.
1781, Nov 13,	Gilchrist, Matthew and Elizabeth Crouch.
1784, Nov 9,	Gillmor, Moses and Isabella Wallace.
1774, Jun 15,	Gowdie, John and Abigail Ryan.
1776, Nov 28,	Goorly, John and --- ---.
1773, --- --,	Graham, John and Sarah Brown.
1779, --- --,	Gray, John and Mary Robinson.
1779, Nov 11,	Gray, Joseph and --- ---.
1783, Feb 25,	Green, Joseph and Sarah Auld.
1772, Apr 1,	Hamilton, Hugh and Ann Campbell.
1788, Sep 27,	Hamilton, Thomas and Mary Kyle.
1795, Jun 11,	Hamilton, William and Rachel Boyd.
1768, Jun 2,	Harris, James and Mary Laird.
1779, May 27,	Harris, James and --- ---.
1749, May 3,	Harris, John Jr. and Elizabeth McClure.
1752, Oct 4,	Harris, William Augustus and Margaret

	Simpson.
1766, Dec --,	Hays, John and Eleanor Elder.
1787, Nov 20	Henderson, James and Margaret Wiggins.
1771, Jan 24,	Hetherington, Alexander and --- ---.
1790, Feb 5,	Hill, Samuel and Nancy Beatty.
1776, Dec 10,	Hodge, Isaac and Margaret Wilson.
1786, Jun 13,	Hutchinson, Joseph and Sarah Cathcart.
1780, Jun 29,	Hutchinson, Samuel and Jane Rutherford.
1799, Nov 26,	Ingram, James and Margaret Logan.
1784, Jun 7,	Irwin, Christopher and Mary Fulk.
1783, May 12,	Jackson, Edward and Margaret Lewis.
1776, Jul 3,	Jenkins, Walter and --- ---.
1774, Mar 31,	Johnson, Alexander and --- ---.
1771, Aug 15,	Johnson, James and --- ---.
1774, -- --,	Kearsley, Samuel and Sarah ---.
1796, Feb 4,	Kelso, John and Sally Morton.
1757, May 23,	Kelso, William and --- Simpson.
1775, Jan 17,	Kennedy, David and --- ---.
1784, Oct 21,	Keys, Robert and Elizabeth Cowden.
1782, Dec 31,	King, Richard and Mary Wylie.
1800, Apr 24,	Kirk, James and Mary Forster.
1777, Dec 23,	Kyle, James and Eleanor Carothers.
1799, Mar 9,	Lanning, John and Catharine Vought.
1778, Sep 10,	Laird, James and --- ---.
1778, Feb 12,	Laird, James and Mary McFarland.
1791, Apr 4,	Laird, John and Rachel ---.
1774, Sep 29,	Lerkin, John and --- ---.
1782, May 6,	Lewis, John and --- ---.
1800, May 29,	Lockhart, Reuben and Peggy Forster.
1780, Jul 20,	Lytle, John and --- ---.
1796, Sep 22,	Lytle, Samuel and Nancy Robinson.
1773, Nov 10,	Maclay, Samuel and Elizabeth Plumket.
1774, Sep 15,	Maclay, William and Mary Harris.
1778, Apr 9,	McAllister, Archibald and --- Hays.
1752, Jun 1,	McChesney, William and Esther (Say) Harris.
1783, Jan 23,	McCleaster, James and Sarah Roan.
1775, Jan 31,	McClure, Andrew, and --- ---.
1782, Aug 8,	McClure, Francis and --- ---.
1779, Aug 3,	McClure, Joseph and --- ---.
1777, Mar 23,	McClure, Richard and --- ---.

1781, Dec 11,	McCord, Samuel and Martha McCormick.
1774, Mar 15,	McCormick, James and Isabella Dixon.
1784, Mar 29,	McCormick, William and Grizel Porter.
1773, --- --,	McCullom, Alexander and Mary Calhoun.
1784, Jun 8,	McDonald, John and Lydia Sturgeon.
1787, May 1,	McElhenny, William and Elizabeth McNeal.
1772, May 7,	McFadden, James and --- ---.
1781, Feb 27,	McGuire, Richard and Eleanor Gilchrist.
1778, Jun 4,	McHadden, William and --- ---.
1778, Dec 10,	McKinzie, James and Mary King.
1771, May 9,	McNair, Thomas and Ann Maria Wallace.
1776, May 7,	McNamara, James and --- ---.
1779, Apr 12,	McQuown, (McEwen) John and --- ---.
1779, Sep 23,	McTeer, Samuel and --- Quigley.
1781, Apr 12,	Maxwell, John and Mary Houston.
1779, Apr 15,	Means, Adam and --- ---.
1776, Apr 25,	Miller, Thomas and --- ---.
1787, Apr 3,	Mitchel, David and Susanna Wilson.
1770, --- --,	Montieth, James and Magaret Maxwell.
1771, May 3o,	Montgomery, James and --- ---.
1775, Apr 18,	Moody, Robert and Margaret Hutchison.
1779, Sep 14,	Moore, William and --- Boyd.
1797, Apr 6,	Morrison, John, Esq. and Flora McCord.
1786, Dec 19,	Murray, Patrick and Mary Brereton Beatty.
1781, Apr 3,	Patterson, John and Jane Johnston.
1776, Oct 15,	Patton, Samuel and --- ---.
1777, Apr 22,	Pinkerton, David and --- ---.
1749, Jun 3,	Plunket, William and Esther Harris.
1785, Mar 7,	Polk, James Smith and Jean Fullion.
1796, Feb 3,	Priestley, William and Peggy Foulke.
1774, Apr 21,	Ramsey, David and --- ---.
1787, Mar 13,	Ramsey, David and Martha Graham.
1782, Apr 8,	Ramsey, Hugh and Margaret McHargue.
1782, Mar 31,	Reid, James and --- ---.
1769, Feb 16,	Reid, John and --- ---.
1771, Jul 15,	Reid, Thomas and Mary West.
1771, Jun 27,	Rhea, Robert and --- ---.
1769, Sep 12,	Robinson, Andrew and --- ---.
1769, Sep 12,	Robinson, James and Martha Cochran.
1781, Mar 1,	Robinson, James and --- Boyce.

1772, Feb 6,	Rodgers, William and --- ---.
1796, Jun 7,	Russell, James and Frances Moore.
1782, May 14,	Russell, Samuel and --- ---.
1772, Jan 2,	Rutherford, James and Margaret Brisban.
1762, --- --,	Rutherford, John and Margaret Park.
1776, Mar 14,	Rutherford, Samuel and Susan Collier.
1774, Aug 13,	Ryan, John and Jane Gowdie.
1778, Mar 11,	Sawyer, Joseph and Elizabeth McFarland.
1781, Dec 18,	Sawyer, William and Mary Sawyer.
1772, May 11,	Shaw, James and --- ---.
1781, Mar 8,	Shearl, John and Margaret Thom.
1776, May 7,	Simpson, John and Margaret Murray.
1774, Feb 10,	Simpson, Mathias and --- ---.
1784, Nov 9,	Sinclair, Duncan and Hannah Templeton.
1771, Jan 31,	Simpson, Thomas and --- ---.
1789, Mar 3,	Sloan, Samuel and Prudence Walker.
1769, May 15,	Smith, William and --- ---.
1793, Mar 7,	Smith, Thomas and Anna Moore.
1776, Jan 12,	Snodgrass, John and --- ---.
1782, May 9,	Spence, James and --- ---.
1782, Jan 31,	Smiley, Thomas and Ann Tucker.
1779, Dec 23,	Sterrett, William, Jr. --- ---.
1782, Apr 1,	Swan, Hugh and --- ---.
1775, Dec 19,	Swan, William and Martha Renick.
1780, --- --,	Taggart, Robert and Mary Simpson.
1776, Jun 25,	Templeton, --- and --- ---.
1785, Mar 15,	Templeton, Robert and Mary Boyd.
1772, May 18,	Thompson, James and --- ---.
1777, Jun 19,	Thompson, John and --- ---.
1776, Apr 9,	Thompson, Samuel and --- ---.
1778, Apr 30,	Todd, James and Mary Wilson.
1774, Aug 25,	Trousdale, John and --- ---.
1781, Jun 21,	Trousdale, William and Elizabeth Glen.
1782, Aug 19,	Vandyke, Lambert and --- ---.
1776, Jan 25,	Walker, James and Barbara McArthur.
1787, Jun 19,	Wallace, James and Sarah Elder.
1770, --- --,	Wallace, Moses and Jean Fulton.
1775, Sep 19,	Wallace, William and --- ---.
1779, Nov 15,	Watson, David and --- ---.
1778, Jun 22,	Weir, Samuel and --- ---.

1788, Jan 13,	White, Thomas and Jean Spence.
1784, Apr 15,	Williams, George and Ann Meloy.
1774, Jun 16,	Wilson, Alexander and Grizel Fulton.
1785, Apr 28,	Wilson, Alexander and Elizabeth Carson.
1772, Apr 30,	Wilson, Hugh and Isabella Fulton.
1745, Apr 3,	Wilson, James and Martha Sterrett.
1776, Feb 13,	Wilson, James and --- ---.
1784, May 18,	Wilson, James and Mary Elder.
1777, Apr 8,	Wilson, Joseph and Margaret Boyd.
1783, Mar 11,	Wilson, Joseph Margaret Boyd.
1773, --- --,	Wilson, William and Elizabeth Robinson.
1777, Jan 23,	Wray, David and Mary Cowden.
1776, Apr 14,	Wylie, James and --- ---.
1786, Dec 19,	Wylie, John and Sarah Whitley.
1777, Jul 31,	Wylie, Thomas and --- ---.
1772, Jun 16,	Young, Andrew and --- ---.
1781, May 10,	Young, William and Martha Wilson.

FETTERHOFF'S (ST. PETER'S) LUTHERAN AND REFORMED CHURCH

Christian of Jacob Baker and Elisabeth, b. 3/20/1789; bapt. 7/18/1790.
Spon: parents.

Henrich of Johannes Baumann (Bowman) and Margareth, b.
10/2/1793; bapt. 11/10/1793. Spon: Georg Schafer and wife, Maria.

Eva of Joh. Nicolaus and Eva Boyer, b. 6/27/1792; confirmed
9/23/1809. Spon: parents.

Elisabeth of Johannes and Magdalena Braun (Brown); bapt.
8/29/1792. Spon: Johan Zimmerman and wife, Elisabeth.

Sarah of Johannes and Magdalena Braun (Brown), b. 8/18/1790; bapt.
9/12/1791. Spon: Johannes Bayer and wife, Catharin.

Ludwig of Ludwig and Catharina Cassel, b. 8/13/1794; bapt.
5/25/1794. Spon: parents

Elisabeth of Johannes and Susanna Dunckel, b. 3/11/1792; bapt.
5/20/1702. Spon: John Miller and wife, Elisabeth.

Johann Conrath of Philip and Appoloni Enders, b. 5/18/1788; bapt.
6/8/1788. Spon: parents

Daniel of Catharina Enders, single, b. 3/19/1790; bapt. 8/15/1790.
Spon: mother.

Susanna of Philip and Elisabeth Enders, b. 6/25/1791; bapt. 10/3/1791.
Spon: Elisabeth Enders, single.

Johannes of Philip and Elisabeth Enders, b. 8/25/1792; bapt.
11/1/1792. Spon: Henrich Tschop and wife, Magdalena.

Margreta of Abraham and Cathrina Etgen, b. 7/10/1798; bapt.
8/26/1798. Spon: Philipp Etgen and wife, Elisabeth.

Johannes Faber, b. 12/6/1776; bapt. 7/18/1819 and wife, Catharine, b.
1/5/1775; bapt. 7/18/1819.

Catharine of John Freeburn and wife, b. 5/10/1796; bapt. 8/30/1807.

Merthe of John Freeburn and wife, b. 2/28/1798; bapt. 8/30/1807.

Mary of John Freeburn and wife, b. 7/21/1799; bapt. 8/30/1807.

Daniel of John Freeburn and wife, b. 11/7/1802; bapt. 8/30/1807.

Elizabeth of John Freeburn and wife, b. 12/8/1806; bapt. 8/30/1807.

Henrich of Friedrich and Barbara Hetzler, b. 11/21/1790; bapt.
5/22/1792. Spon: G. Adam Fritz and Elizabeth.

Johann Balthaser of Friedrich and Barbara Hetzler, b. 6/12/1786;
bapt. 6/8/1788. Spon: parents.

Johannes of Friedrich and Barbara Hetzler, b. 11/18/1787; bapt.

6/8/1788. Spon: Maria Zimmerman.

Catharina of Gottlieb and Maria Kline (Klein), b. 10/15/1787; bapt. 6/8/1788. Spon: Andreas Schweigert and Cath. Harman, single.

Regina of Gottlieb and Maria Kline (Klein), b. 1/20/1790; bapt. 4/25/1790. Spon: parents.

Catharina of Georg and Catharina Kurtz, b. 7/23/1789; bapt. 8/9/1789. Spon: Philip Enders and Catharina Herman, single.

Johannes of Adam and Catharina Laudermilch, b. 5/6/1788; bapt. 6/8/1788. Spon: Ludwig Schott and wife, Catharina.

Johan Ludwig of Andreas Messershmidt and Eva, b. 8/26/1787; bapt. 6/8/1788. Spon: Ludwig Schallman and wife, Elisabeth.

Johann Georg of Andreas Messershmidt and Eva, b. 8/31/1790; bapt. 3/27/1791. Spon: George Shafer, married.

Henrich of Andreas Messershmidt and Eva, b. 8/31/1790; bapt. 3/27/1791. Spon: Johannes Schweigart and Elisabeth Fritz, single.

Johann Jacob of Andreas Messershmidt and Eva; bapt. 8/19/1792. Spon: Johan Urich and wife.

Joseph of Jost Miller and Elisabeth, b. 8/6/1787; bapt. 6/8/1788. Spon: parents.

Anna Catharine of Heinrich Paul and Margareth, b. 2/11/1790; bapt. 3/27/1791. Spon: Peter Schweigert and wife.

Johannes of Heinrich Paul and Margareth, b. 10/10/1792; bapt. 1/6/1793. Spon: parents.

Elisabeth of Georg Schaffer (Shaffer) and Maria, b. 5/28/1791; bapt. 6/19/1791. Spon: Michael Bauer and wife, Veronica.

Johann Wilhelm of Philipp Schott (Shott) and Catharina, b. 11/2/1798; bapt. 4/28/1799. Spon: Peter Schott and wife, Magdalene.

Johann Michael of Adam Schweigart (Sweigard) and Maria, b. 11/4/1790; bapt. 1/30/1791. Spon: Michael Gottshall and wife, Catharine.

Anna Barbara of Peter Schweigart (Sweigard) and Maria, b. 12/16/1792; bapt. 1/6/1793. Spon: Margareth Schopp, single.

Johann Peter of Peter Schweigart (Sweigard) and Maria, b. 6/26/1795; bapt. 6/19/1795. Spon: Adam Schweigart and wife, Maria.

Anna Maria of Johannes Schweigart (Sweigard) and Anna, b. 6/8/1795; bapt. 3/31/1795. Spon: Adam Schweigart and wife, Maria.

Johann Georg of Johannes Schweigart (Sweigard) and Anna, b. 6/8/1795; bapt. 6/29/1795. Spon: George Schaefer and wife, Maria.

Daniel of Johann Schweigart (Sweigard) and Maria, b. 8/17/1793; bapt. 9/15/1793. Spon: parents.

James of James Tratter and Margaretha, b. 2/7/1788; bapt. 6/8/1788. Spon: Gottlieb Klein.

Elisabeth of James Tratter and Margaretha, b. 8/7/1790; bapt. 1/30/1791. Spon: Adam Schweigert and wife, Maria.

Eva Maria Enders of Anna Maria Zimmerman, widow, b. 3/20/1791; bapt. 5/22/1791. Spon: Eva Maria Edners; single.

Catharina of Johannes Zimmerman and Elisabeth, b. 2/4/1791; bapt. 7/11/1791. Spon: Jost. Miller and wife Elisabeth.

Henrich of Johannes and Elisabeth Zimmerman, b. 7/3/1792; bapt. 8/18/1792. Spon: John Braun and wife, Magdalena.

Susanna of Johannes and Elisabeth Zimmerman, b. 4/3/1794; bapt. 5/25/1794. Spon: Christian Zimmerman and Catharine Bauerman, single.

Catharina Elisabeth of Friederich Zimmerman and Catharina, b. 6/29/1795. Spon: Philipp Schott and wife, Elisabeth.

Maria Magdalena of Adam Zimmerman and Magdalena, b. 8/12/1792; bapt. 9/16/1792. Spon: Jacob Braun and wife, Eva Maria.

Anna Catharine of Adam Zimmerman and Magdalena, b. 2/26/1798; bapt. 3/22/1798. Spon: Friedrich Zimmerman and wife, Catharine.

SAINT PAUL'S EVANGELICAL LUTHERAN CHURCH

Baptisms in church in Derry Township

Elisabeta of Joann Conrad Wölfflin; b. Oct 14, 1757; bapt. Oct 8, 1757. Spon: Jacob Lentz and wife.

Jo. Georg of Joann Armbruster, b. Sep 24, 1757; bapt. same day. Spon: Georg Steuer and wife.

Christina of J. Deiss, b. Oct 3, 1757; bapt. same day. Spon: Georg Bumbach and wife,

Jo. Georg of Daniel Braun, b. Sep 2, 1757; bapt. same day. Spon: J. Georg Schüz and his sister.

Joannes Dietrich, illegitimate, of Joannes Wunderlich, b. Nov 11, 1757; bapt. Dec 4, 1757. Spon: J. Dietrich Morell and wife.

Philipp Jacob of Conrad Wölffle, b. Jan 24, 1759; bapt. Feb 25, 1759. Spon: Philipp Fischer.

Joannes of Daniel Braun, b. Aug 20, 1759; bapt. Nov 4, 1759. Spon: J. Casseel and wife.

SAINT PAUL'S EVANGELICAL LUTHERAN CHURCH 67

Joannes of J. Deiss, b. Nov 29, 1758. Spon: J. Neukommer and wife.
Joann of Conrad Wölffle, b. Mar 30, 1760; bapt. Apr 20, 1760. Spon:
Jacob Lenz and wife.
Johs. Henrich of Henrich Krieger and wife, b. Jan 18; bapt. Feb 1,
1773. Spon: Hen. Ditzel and wife (Enderlein).
Anna Maria of Fridrich Staal and wife, Mar. Elisabeth, b. Jun 10,
1771; bapt. Jul 10, 1771. Spon: Henrich Fritz and Anna Maria
(Enderlein).
Mattheus of Frid. Staal and wife, Elisabeth, b. Nov 2, 1772; bapt. Jan
3, 1773. Spon: grandparents, Mr. Staal (Enderlein).
Elisabeth of Margaretha Fischborinin, b. Apr 24; bapt. May 20, 1773.
Spon: Henrich Ditzel and wife, Catharina (Enderlein).
Jacob Fritrig of Fritrig Stall and Elisabetha, b. Jun 10, 1774. Spon:
Jacob Keterring and wife Margareth.
Maximilian of Fritrig Stall and Elisabetha, b. Aug 4, 1776. Spon:
Maximilian Speidel and wife, Margaretha (Stoever).
Anna Maria of Jacob Lentz, b. Nov 28, 1757; bapt. Jan 29, 1758.
Spon: Jacob Schütz and wife; Anna Maria Lentzin.
Sussanna of Maxmilian Speidel, Jr., b. Jan 9, 1771; bapt. Jan 13,
1771. Spon: Friedrich Eberhard and Elisabetha, single persons
(Enderlein).
Maxmilian of Maxmilian Speidel, Jr., b. Mar 19, 1772; bapt. Mar 22,
1772. Spon: Maximilian Speitel, Sr. and wife, Margareth
(Enderlein) [This should probably be Speidel]
Jacob of Maxmilian Speidel, Jr., b. Oct 17, 1773; bapt. Nov 14, 1773.
Spon: Jacob Kettenring, single and Margareth Speitelin, single.
(Enderlein)
Johannes of Maxmilian Speidel, Jr., b. Apr 14, 1776; bapt. Apr 21,
1776. Spon: Peter Buchs and his wife, Margaretha. (Stoever)
Elisabetha of Maxmilian Speidel, Jr., b. Jan 14, 1778. Spon: Jacob
Speidell and Elisabetha.
Johan Jorg of Maxmilian Speidel, Jr., b. Aug 22, 1779. Spon: Jorg
Freÿ and wife, Katria [sic].
Johan Peter of Maxmilian Speidel, Jr., b. Apr 13, 1781. Spon: Peter
Buchs and wife, Margaretha.
Georg of Peter Spengler, b. Jan 15, 1758; bapt. Feb 26, 1758. Spon:
Georg Bombach and wife.
Catharina Elisabetha of Joann Hennrich Oetzel, b. Jan 26, 1758;
bapt. Jan 29, 1758; d. May 20, 1758. Spon: Philipp Fischborn and
his wife.

Joann Adam of Jacob Speidel, b. Feb 11, 1762; bapt. Easter Sunday, 1762. Spon: Joann Adam Schneider and wife.

Maria Elisabetha of Jacob Speidel, b. Feb 28, 1763; bapt. Mar 8, 1763. Spon: Joann Haunschen and wife.

Margaretha of Jacob Speidel, b. Feb 24, 1767; bapt. Mar 23, 1767. Spon: Fridrich Stahl and Margaretha Speidel.

Maxmilian of Jacob Speidel, b. Feb 22, 1770; bapt. Mar 1, 1770. Spon: Maxmilian Speidel and his wife Margaretha (Enderlein).

Johannes of Jacob Speidel, b. Dec 6, 1776. Spon: Peter Buchs and wife Markert. [marked with a cross, meaning the child died.]

Jacob of Jacob Speidel, b. b. Feb 15, 1777. Spon: Max Speidel and wife, Barra.

Christina of Jacob Speidel, b. Jul 17, 1779. Spon: Fritrig Stall and wife, Elisabetha.

Johannes and Georg, twins, of Jacob Speidel, b. Jan 22, 1782; bapt. Feb 17, 1782. Spon: Maxmilian Speidel and Barbara, Philip Bliss and Magdalena Speidel. (Melsheimer).

George Nicolaus of Christian Allemann, b. Jan 16, 1758; bapt. Feb 26, 1758. Spon: Georg Frey and wife; Nicolaus Stauch and wife.

Herman Hennrich of Christian Allemann, b. Apr 15, 1759; bapt. Apr 29, 1759. Spon: George Fey [sic] and wife.

Catharina of Christian Allemann, b. Feb 14, 1761; bapt. Mar 22, 1761. Spon: Georg Frey and wife.

Catarina Magdalena of Johannes Braun, b. Feb 25, 1758; bapt. Mar 26, 1758. Spon: Michael Gensel and wife; Jerg Frejen's wife.

Susanna of William Duen, b. Nov 10, 1754. Spon: Stolfel Manz and wife.

Vincenz of Joan Braun, b. Oct 4, 1757; bapt. Oct 8, 1758. Spon: Vincenz Kieffer and wife.

Catarina Elisabeta of Philipp Genter, b. Jan 25, 1758; bapt. Oct 8, 1758. Spon: Philipp Fischborn and wife.

Johan Peter of Philipp Genter, b. Dec 9, 1760; bapt. Dec 28, 1760. Spon: Peter Gunther and wife.

Anna Regina of Jacob Albrecht, b. Apr 10, 1756. Spon: Frantz Neukometer.

Joann Philipp of Jacob Albrecht, b. Jul 10, 1758; bapt. Sep 10, 1758. Spon: Philipp Partemer and Anna Maria Etzweilerin.

Joann Christoph of Jacob Albrecht, b. Nov 20, 1758; bapt. Dec 25, 1760. Spon: Stolfel Schub and wife.

Joann Peter of Jacob Albrecht, b. Aug 16, 1761; bapt. Sep 6, 1761.

Spon: Joann Peter Gunter and wife.

Jacob of Jacob Albrecht, b. Dec 26, 1764. Spon: Antonj Blessle and wife.

Christina of Jacob Albrecht, b. May 15, 1767; bapt. Jun 12, 1767. Spon: Mathaeus Stahl and wife.

Margareta of Jonas Le Ruh, b. Sep 29, 1757; bapt. Oct 8, 1757. Spon: Joannes Neukommer and wife.

Joann Philipp of Joann Borresch, b. Mar 14, 1758; bapt. May 21, 1758. Spon: Philipp Gunther and wife.

Catharina of Joann Borresch, b. Jan 2, 1760; bapt. Dec 25, 1759 [sic should read 1760]. Spon: Philipp Fischborn and wife.

Joann Fridrich of Joann Borresch, b. Feb 18, 1762; bapt. Estomihi Sunday, 1762.

J. Adam of Michael Gänsle, b. May 18, 1758; bapt. May 21, 1758. Spon: Adam Delker and wife.

Joann Christoff of Mechior Flennspach, b. May 27, 1758; bapt. Jun 18, 1758. Spon: Stolfel Schipp and wife.

Barbara of Fridrich Forster, b. Mar 8, 1759; bapt. May 29, 1759. Spon: Philip Fischer.

Philipp Fridrich of Fridrich Forster, b. Feb 26, 1761; bapt. Mar 22, 1761. Spon: Philipp Fischer and wife.

Joann Hennrich of Fridrich Forster, b. Feb 17, 1763; bapt. Apr 2, 1763. Spon: Hennrich Scheffer and wife.

Mattaeus of Michael Huber, Jr., b. Apr 18, 1757. Spon: Mattaeus Weimer and wife.

Margaretha of Matheis Stoll, b. Apr 4, 1759; bapt. Apr 29, 1759. Spon: Maximilian Speidel and wife.

Joann Fridrich of Fridrich Hummel, b. Oct 5, 1758; bapt. Oct 8, 1758. Spon: Joann Adam Kettering and wife.

Eva of Fridrich Hummel, b. Nov 7, 1756; bapt. not long after. Spon: Simon Brez and Eva Oberlin.

Antonj of Fridrich Hummel, b. Jan 9, 1761; bapt. Jan 25, 1761. Spon: Antonj Blessle and wife.

Anna Catharina of Michael Cassel, b. Oct 5, 1758; bapt. Nov 9, 1758. Spon: Fridrich Cassel and Anna Weimerin.

Fridrich of Michael Cassel, b. Aug 26, 1759. Spon: Fridrich Cassel and Anna Weimerin.

Joann Michael of Michael Cassel, b. May 24, 1761; bapt. 4th Sunday after Trinity. Spon: Jacob Lenz and wife.

Georg Jacob of Jacob Baumann, b. Oct 16, 1758; bapt. Nov 8, 1758.

Spon: Georg Gros and wife. (born after death of the father.)

Christina of Gottlieb David Ettelin, b. Jul 24, 1752; bapt. Dec 31, 1752. Spon: Michael Kehsinger and Cat. Marg. Schallin (?).

J. Philipp of Gottlieb David Ettelin, b. Apr 22, 1755. Spon: Ulrich Hübscher and wife.

Conrad of Gottlieb David Ettelin, b. May 31, 1757. Spon: Conrad Wölffle and wife.

Catharina Elisabeta of Gottlieb David Ettelin, b. Mar 8, 1759. Spon: Philipp Fischborn and wife.

David of Gottlieb David Ettelin, b. Jan 30, 1760; bapt. Estomihi Sunday, 1762. Spon: Georg Frey and wife.

Anna Margaretha of Joseph Germanne, b. May 15, 1759; bapt. Jun 17, 1759. Spon: Fridrich Morell and wife.

Catharina Elisabeta of Joseph Germanne, b. Mar 28, 1765; bapt. Apr 16, 1765. Spon: Hennrich Ditzel and wife.

Juliana of Joseph Germanne, b. Dec 8, 1761; bapt. the next Sunday. Spon: Joannes Carbine and wife.

Margareta of Ludwig Trabler, b. Jun 12, 1759; bapt. same day. Spon: Jo. Philipp Gunter.

Georg Fridrich and Joann Philipp, two boys of Christoph Sesupp, b. May 27, 1759; bapt. Jun 17, 1759. Spon: Fridrich Hummel and wife; Philip Partemer and wife.

Philip Fridrich of Christoph Sesupp, b. Jul 12, 1760; bapt. 10th Sun after Trinity. Spon: Philip Partemer and wife; Fridrich Hummel and wife.

Margareta of Jacob Zeitter, b. May 19, 1754. Spon: Philipp Gunter and wife.

J. Jacob of Jacob Zeitter, b. Sep 20, 1757. Spon: Jacob Albrecht and wife.

Maria Christina of Jacob Zeitter, b. Nov. 8, no year given. Spon: Willm Strickler and wife.

Joannes of Jacob Zeitter, b. Jun 20, 1762; bapt. Estomihi, 1762. Spon: Joan Boretsch and wife.

Georg Fridrich of Antonj Blessle, b. Nov 1, 1759; bapt. Dec 27, 1759. Spon: Fridrich Hummel and wife.

Antonius of Antonj Blessle, b. Mar 27, 1762. Spon: Anton Hemberle and wife.

Christian of Antonj Blessle, b. Nov 29, 1765. Spon: Anton Carbine and wife.

J. Michael of Michael Boltz, b. Jul 22, 1758. Spon: Andreas Vel and wife.

Jacob Fridrich of Michael Boltz, b. Mar 2, 1760; bapt. Judica Sunday. Spon: Georg Jacob Boltz and Catarina Majerin.

Samuel of Joannes Küstler, b. Mar 29, 1759. Spon: Fridrich Hummel and wife.

Fridrich of Joannes Küstler, b. Mar 15, 1761; bapt. Laetare, 1761. Spon: Fridrich Hummel and wife.

A dau. of Michael Danckmann, b. Mar 3, 1760; bapt. Third Sunday after Trinity, 1761. Spon: Joann Cassel and wife.

Maria Margareta of Philipp Fischborn, b. Jul 24, 1753. Spon: Philipp Boltz and wife.

Joann Philipp of Philipp Fischborn, b. Nov 15, 1754. Spon: Philip Fischborn and wife, in whose absence Wenceslaus Boltz served as proxy.

Ludwig of Philipp Fischborn, b. Sep 3, 1756. Spon: Ludovicus Boltz and wife.

Joann Dietrich of Philipp Fischborn, b. Jun 29, 1760; bapt. Trinity VI, 1760. Spon: Jo Dietrich Morell and wife.

Joann Peter of Philipp Fischborn, b. Apr 16, 1758. Spon: Peter Ales and Maria Hoffmaennin.

Antony of Philipp Fischborn, b. Jun 1, 1762; bapt. Jul 4, 1762. Spon: Antony Cehler and wife.

Maria Magdalena of Philipp Fischborn, b. Feb 10, 1765; bapt. a few days afterward. Spon: Peter Gunther and wife.

Catharine Elisabeta of Philipp Fischborn, b. Aug 12, 1767; bapt. Trinity VI, 1767. Spon: Hennrich Dietzel and wife.

Magdalena of Hennrich Majer, b. Nov 25, 1757; bapt. Trinity VI, 1760. Spon: Fridrich Cassel, Magdalena Küstlerin.

Hennrich of Hennrich Majer, b. Dec 20, 1759; bapt. Trinity VI, 1760. Spon: Nicobus Cassel and Anna Maria Schefferin.

Georg Fridrich of Joannes Cassel, b. Jul 28, 1760; bapt. Aug 10, 1760. Spon: Fridrich Hummel and wife.

Joann Philipp of Antonj Kermänne, b. Dec 2, 1758. Spon: Philipp Fischborn and wife.

Joannes of Antonj Kermänne, b. Jun 15, 1760; bapt. Jul 13, 1760. Spon: Joannes Kermänne.

Antoni of Antonj Kermänne, b. Nov 14, 1764. Spon: Antonius Blessle and wife.

Joann Martin of Antonj Kermänne, b. Sep 12, 1766; bapt. Oct 4, 1766. Spon: Joann Martin Collmer and wife.

Joann Philipp of Philipp Partemer, b. Dec 16, 1760; bapt. Jan 25, 1761. Spon: Philipp Fischborn and wife.

Antoni of Philip Blessle and wife, Magdalena, b. Apr 25, 1783; bapt. May 18, 1783. Spon: Antony Blessle and wife,Salome. [Melsheimer].

Joannes of ? McKallens, b. Jun 10, 1761; bapt. Sep 6, 1761. Spon: Ludwig Traber and wife.

Anna Catarina of Rudolph Haab, b. Apr 18, 1761; bapt. Feast of the Ascension. Spon: Adam Waler and wife.

Maria Elisabeta of Joann Unschild, b. May 20, 1759; bapt. Festival of the Trinity, 1761. Spon: Jacob Speidel and Elisabeta Grebin.

Christina of Joann Unschild, b. Jun 6, 1762; bapt. Sep 9, 1762. Spon: Jacob Speidel and wife.

Andreas of Joann Unschild, b. Oct 3, 1766; bapt. Nov 2, 1766. Spon: Joannes Goetz and Christina Schumacherin.

Rosina of Nicolaus Staud, b. Jun 6, 1761; bapt. 12th Sunday after Trintiy, 176(?).

Elisabeta of Joann Georg Weeber, b. Jan 19, 1761; bapt. Trinity 8, 1761. Spon: Joann Huber and Susanna Scherls.

Susanna of Carolus Willms, b. Sep, 1755; bapt. 8 Trinity 1761. Spon: Joannes Albrecht and wife.

Joann Willhelm of Carolus Willms, b. Apr, 1757. Spon: Jacob Burkhard and Salome Huberin.

Maria Magdalena of Fridrich Cassel, b. Jan 25, 1762; bapt. Estomihi, 1762. Spon: Jacob König and Anna Maria Kessingerin, widow.

Maria Eva of Fridrich Cassel, b. Sep 22, 1762; bapt. Oct 14, 1762. Spon: Michael Cassel and wife.

Joann Jacob of Peter Boks, b. Jun 21. 1761; bapt. May 20, 1763. Spon: Georg Weeber and wife.

Joann Conrad of Peter Boks, b. Aug 4, 1763; bapt. Aug 23, 1763. Spon: Joannes Deiss and wife.

Adam of Adam Majer, b. Apr 9, 1762; bapt. Quasimodo, 1762. Spon: Frid Forster and wife.

Maria Barbara of Ludwig Beel, b. Feb 23, 1762; bapt. Jul 4, 1762. Spon: Dieterich Morell and wife.

Willhelm of Ludwig Beel, b. Aug 24, 1760; bapt. 8 wks after birth. Spon: Ludwig Beel and wife.

Catarina Elisabeta of Anton Oehler, b. Dec 26, 1762 [sic; read 1761]; bapt. Jul 4, 1762. Spon: Philipp Fischborn and wife.

Elisabetha of David Fromm and wife, Rosina, b. Jan 13; bapt. Mar 24,

1776. Spon: Maximilian Speidel, Jr. and wife Catarina Barbara.
[Stoever]

Anna Margaretha of Johann Georg Buchs and wife, Elisabetha, b.
Feb 9; bapt. Mar 24, 1776. Spon: Peter Buchs, Sr. and wife,
Margaretha. (Stoever)

Johann Daniel of Johann Georg Buchs and wife, Elisabetha, b. Aug
22; bapt. Sep 7, 1777. Spon: Johann Daniel and wife, Agnes.
(Stoever)

Joannes of Johann Georg Buchs and wife, Elisabetha, b. Jul 18, 1762;
bapt. Jul 4, 1762. Spon: Joannes Mater and wife.

Anna Margaretha of Johannes Blessing and wife, Catharina; bapt.
Feb 17, 1782. Spon: Antony Blessing and Margaretha Krüger.
(Melsheimer).

Rosina of Georg Bauer, b. Jan 26, 1763; bapt. May 1, 1763. Spon:
Fridrich Hummel and his wife.

Catarina of Georg Huber, b. Apr 10, 1761. Spon: Caspar Huber and
Catharina Ernstin.

Rosina of Georg Huber, b. Mar 27, 1763; bapt. May 1, 1763. Spon:
Joann Cassel and wife.

Joann Peter of Jost Joder, b. Mar 16, 1763; bapt. May 1, 1763. Spon:
Joann Peter Pfannenkuchen and wife.

Catharina Elisabeta of Joannes Carmine, b. Oct 10, 1763; bapt. Nov
6, 1763. Spon: Hennrich Ditzel and wife.

Rebecca of Joannes Carmine, b. Apr 14, 1765; bapt. Feast of the
Ascension, 1765. Spon: Michael Carmine and Rebecca, dau of
Peter Gunther.

Maria Barbara of Joannes Carmine, b. Jul 22, 1766. Spon: Antoniy
Blessle and wife.

Joannes of Joannes Carmine, b. Oct 19, 1767; bapt. Nov 1, 1767.
Spon: Anton Carmene and wife.

Catharina of Wilhelm Kräb and Catharina, b. Oct 29, 1776; bapt. Nov
5, 1776. Spon: Augustinus Stahl and wife, Anna. (Stoever)

Johannes of Wilhelm Kräb and Catharina, b. Aug 19, 1779; bapt. Sep
5, 1779. Spon: Jacob Speidel and wife, Elisabeth. (Melsheimer)

Jacob of Wilhelm Kräb and Catharina, b. Aug 25, 1781; bapt. Sep 9,
1781. Spon: Fried. Stahl and wife, Elisabeth. (Mesheimer)

Joann Philipp of Hennrich Ditzel, b. Jul 6, 1763; bapt. the next
Sunday. Spon: Philipp Fischborn and wife.

Joann Hennrich of Hennrich Ditzel, b. Dec. 25, 1766; bapt. the 28th
of the same mo. Spon: Philipp Fischborn and wife.

Catharina of Hennrich Ditzel, b. Dec 27, 1771; bapt. Jan 6, 1772.
Spon: Joseph Karmenie and wife. (Enderlein)
Johannes of Hennrich Ditzel, b. Oct 26, 1768; bapt. Nov 1, 1768.
Spon: Philipp Fischborn and wife. (Enderlein)
Barbara of Hennrich Ditzel, b. Apr 26, 1773; bapt. Apr 30, 1773.
Spon: Jacob Kettenring and Catharina Weberin, both single
persons. (Enderlein)
Loisa of Joann Hennrich Lampert, b. Aug 30, 1766; bapt. Oct 4, 1766.
Spon: Joann Eberhard Kettenring, Catharina Daudin and Loisa
Guntherin.

Baptisms by Pastor Johan Paul Ferdinand Kramer

Maria Barbara of Georg Schupp and wife, Lowisa, b. Jul 11, 1775;
bapt. Aug 13, 1775. Spon: Johannes Bardemer and Catarina.
(Stoever)
Elisabetha of Georg Schupp and wife, Lowisa, b. Feb 20, 1777; bapt.
Mar 23, 1777. Spon: Christoph Schupp and Anna Margaretha.
(Stoever)
Daniel Schupp of Georg Schupp and wife, Lowisa, b. Dec 28, 1778;
bapt. Feb 21, 1779. Spon: father and mother. (Melsheimer)
Maria Sara of Georg Schupp and wife, Lowisa, b. Jan 17, 1782; bapt.
Mar 29, 1782. Spon: Christoph Schupp and wife, Rosina.
(Melsheimer)
Christina of Augustinus Stahl and Anna Elisabetha, b. Jul 21, 1775;
bapt. Sep 10, 1775. Spon: Wilhelm Kröp and Catarina. (Stoever)
Johannes of Johannes Bucks and wife, Margaretha, b. Sep 7, 1779;
bapt. Dec 1, 1779. Spon: Peter Buchs and wife. (Melsheimer)
Elisabeth of Johannes Bucks and wife, Margaretha, b. Aug 9, 1781;
bapt. Sep 7, 1781. Spon: Jacob Buchs and Elisab. Bauer.
(Melsheimer)
Johan Peter of Johannes Bucks and wife, Margaretha, b. Aug 9, 1783;
bapt. Sep 14, 1783. Spon: Peter Bucks and wife. (Melsheimer)
Marialiesabet of Matdes Senger, b. Nov 11; bapt. Dec 13, 1788.
Susanna Rudin, b. May 27, 1789.
Magdalena Sengerin, b. Sep 3, 1789; bapt. Sep 26.
Susanna Bretzin of Andon Bretz, b. Oct 3, 1789; bapt. Nov 29.
Magdalena Senger of Conrath Senger and his wife, b. Sep 3, 1789;
bapt. Sep 26, 1789.
Philip Mich. b. Feb 25, 1790. Spon: Machsmilianus Speidel and wife.
Susanna Schmidtin of Johannes Schmid, b. Jun 23, 1792; bapt. Mar

11.

Johan Peter Büx b. Sep 2; bapt. Nov 5, 1787. Spon: Johann Peter Bocks and wife.

Johannes Schefer was born.

Chaterina of Chunrod Senger and wife, Chaterina b. Dec 13, (1787); bapt. Mar 30, 1788.

Eliesabeta of Willhelm Speidel and wife, Sawina, b. Mar 5; bapt. Mar 30, 1788.

Jacob of Johannes Bucks and wife, Margareda, b. Sep 20, (1787); bapt. Mar 30, 1788.

Johannes of Jacob Miller and wife, Christdinna, b. Mar 15, 1788.

Sallme of Andreas Herauf and wife, Eliesabeta, b. Mar 20, 1788.

Johan Görg of Jacob Speidel and wife, b. May 15, 1788; bapt. May 25, 1788.

A dau. of Johann Görg Bucks, b. Apr 30, 1788; bapt. May 25.

Daniel Speittel of Maximilianus Speidel and wife, Barbara, b. May 21, 1788; bapt. Jun 16. Spon: Augustdinnes Stahl and wife, Anna.

Anamaria of Jacob Bucks and wife, Anamaria, b. Dec 25, 1788; bapt. Jan 4, (1789).

Barbara Grebin, b. Apr 23, 1789; bapt. May 16, 1789.

Ana Stalin, b. Apr 26, 1789; bapt. May 26, 1789.

Barbara ---, b. Feb 2, 1788; bapt. May 16, 1789.

Johan Fielip Tidtrig, b. Jan 3, 1789; bapt. Jun 7, 1789.

Christina ---, b. Aug 15, 1789; bapt. Jun 7, (1789).

A son of Christian Nol and wife, b. Feb 4, 1791; bapt. Jun 27.

Gorg Fridrig of Jacob Bucks and wife, b. Oct 17, 1790; bapt. Oct 24, 1790.

A dau. of Chunrath Senger and wife, b. Jul 27, 1791; bapt. Sep 11.

A dau. of Nicklaus Spring and wife, b. Sep 18, 1791; bapt. Nov 13.

Magdalena of Wielhelm Speidel, b. Feb 14, 1792; bapt. Feb 19.

Baptisms in the Maxe Church (Maxenkirch)
by George Lochman, Evang. Luth. Preacher

Johan Jacob of Jacob Buks and wife, b. Nov 5, 1794; bapt. Nov 30, 1794. Spon: Peter Buks and wife.

Christian Friedrich of Henrich Schlotterbeck and wife, b. not given; bapt. Nov 30, 1794. Spon: Christian Mitschel.

Jonathan of Abraham Kopp and wife, b. Dec 8, 1794; bapt. Dec 26, 1794. Spon: Christian Bleslÿ and wife.

Friedrich of Christian Bleslÿ, b. Nov 29, 1794; bapt. Dec 26, 1794.

Spon: Friedrich Bickel and wife.

Allexander of Andreas Mayer and Dorothea, b. Feb 9, 1795; bapt. May 2, 1795. Spon: parents.

Christian of Jacob Speidel and Susanna, b. Apr 2, 1795; bapt. May 2, 1795. Spon: Christian Mitschel and wife.

Fronica of Thomas Moore and wife, b. not given; bapt. May 2, 1795. Spon: Peter Buks and wife.

Peter of Abraham Gephart and wife, b. Dec 14, 1794; bapt. May 2, 1795. Spon: parents.

Johan Jacob of Abraham Lohrman and wife, b. Dec 7, 1794; bapt. May 2, 1795. Spon: Jacob Danbenberger and wife.

Anna Mar. Elisabeth of Conrad Buks and wife, b. Dec, 1794; bapt. Jul 12. 1795. Spon: Max. Bucks and wife.

James of Robert Ringle and wife, b. Jan 8, 1793; bapt. Jul 12, 1795. Spon: Jacob Rinehart, Jr.

Susanna of Johan Spang and wife, b. not given; bapt. Aug 23, 1795. Spon: Max Speidel and wife.

Abraham of Wilhelm Gräb and wife, b. Aug 7, 1795; bapt. Aug 23, 1795. Spon: Abraham Gephart and wife.

Henrich of Maximilian Buks and wife, b. 3 weeks ago; bapt. Sep 24, 1795. Spon: parents.

Elisabeth of Wilhelm Mäyer and wife, b. 8 weeks ago; bapt. Sep 24, 1795. Spon: Michael Stuckÿ.

Georg of Friedrich Schlotterbeck and wife, b. not given; bapt. Apr 3, 1796. Spon: Philip Blesly and wife.

Christian of Philip Blesly and wife, b. Mar 7, 1796; bapt. Apr 3, 1796. Spon: Christian Blesly and wife.

Justina, illegitimate, b. Mar 22, 1796; bapt. Apr 3, 1796. Spon: --- Fleckin.

Moses of Wilhelm Aaron and wife, b. Apr 2, 1796; bapt. Apr 3, 1796. Spon: Maximilian Speidel and wife.

Margreta of Jacob Bucks and wife, Ann. Maria, b. Jun 25, 1796; bapt. Jul 25, 1796. Spon: Widow Bucksin.

Benjamin of Andreas Mayer and Dorothea, b. Jul 16, 1796; bapt. Sep 3, 1796. Spon: parents.

Michel of Michel Lebküchler and Susanna, b. Dec 2, 1784; bapt. Sep 4, 1796.

Henrich of Michel Lebkühler and Susanna, b. Aug 18, 1786; bapt. Sep 4, 1796.

David of Michel Lebküchler and Susanna, b. Nov 9, 1788; bapt. Sep 4, 1796.

Catarina of Michel Lebküchler and Susanna, b. Sep 11, 1791; bapt. Sep 4, 1796.

Joseph of Michel Lebküchler and Susanna, b. Oct 4, 1793; bapt. Sep 4, 1796.

Johannes of Michel Lebküchler and Susanna, b. Sep 12, 1795; bapt. Sep 4, 1796.

Catarina of Christr. Bodenstein and Elisab., b. Sep 25, 1793; bapt. Sep 4, 1796.

Philip of Christr. Bodenstein and Elisab. b. Jun 3, 1796; bapt. Sep 4, 1796.

Elisabeth of Joh. Ernst and wife, b. Jan 6, 1797; bapt. Apr 3, 1797. Spon: Christoph Ernst and wife . (Hummestown).

Christian of Christian Blessing and Catar. b. Jan 18, 1797; bapt. Apr 3, 1797. Spon: Michael Spad.

Johannes of Anthony Blessing and wife, b. Jan 22, 1797; bapt. Apr 3, 1797. Spon: Philip Blessing.

David of Wilhelm Speidel and wife, b. Oct 8, 1796; bapt. Apr 3, 1797. Spon: Peter Beinhauer and wife.

Johan Philip of Abraham Kop and wife, b. Mar 25, 1797; bapt. May 4, 1797. Spon: Philip Blessing and wife.

Wilhelm Morrison of Christian Kaley and wife, b. Apr 14, 1797; bapt. May 4, 1797. Spon: Jacob Rinehart.

Elisabeth (illegitimate) of Adam Schneider and Mary Davis, b. Jun, 1796; bapt. Sep 17, 1797. Spon: Jacob Kinzel and wife.

--- of David Boden and wife; bapt. Sep 17, 1797. Spon: Johannes Speidel and wife.

--- of Max Bucks and wife; bapt. Sep 17, 1797. Spon: the mother.

Johannes of Johannes Bretz and wife, b. Jan 4, 1798; bapt. Feb 19, 1798. Spon: parents.

Susanna of Friedrich Schlotterbeck and wife, b. Oct 8, 1797; bapt. Feb 19, 1798. Spon: Dorothea James.

John (illegitimate) of Peter Remar, b. Nov, 1797; bapt. Feb 19, 1798. Spon: Johannes Kleber.

Jonas of Jacob Bucks and wife, b. Feb 11, 1798; bapt. Apr 10, 1798. Spon: parents.

David of Aaron Wilhelm and wife, b. Mar 14, 1798; bapt. Jun 1798. Spon: Maximilian Speidel and wife.

Johannes of Christian Kaley and wife, b. Aug 29, 1798; bapt. Sep, 1798. Spon: Jacob Rinehart and wife.

Michael of Philip Blessly and wife, b. Dec 13, 1798; bapt. Dec, 1798. Spon: Michael Spad.

Charles of Patrick McKinney and wife, b. Aug 30, 1798; bapt. Dec, 1798. Spon: Patrick Kearney and Barbara Harvey.

Henrich of Phillip Bollinger and wife, b. Mar, 1799; bapt. May 2, 1799.

Dorothea of Phillip Bollinger and wife, b. Jan, 1798; bapt. May 2, 1799.

Anna Maria of Georg Zeiter and wife, b. Jul 21, 1798; bapt. May 2, 1799. Spon: Henr. Aleman and wife.

Dietrich of Adam Kopach and wife, b. Oct 9, 1798; bapt. May 2, 1799. Spon: Wilhelm Gräb.

Sara of Christian Blesly and wife, b. Jun 15, 1799; bapt. Aug, 1799. Spon: Johannes Schenk and wife.

Catarina of Dietrich Kämmerer and wife, b. Sep 17, 1799; bapt. Dec, 1799. Spon: father.

Joseph of Robert Dunbar and wife, no dates for birth or baptism. Spon: Christian Blesly.

Johannes of Jacob Lang, no dates for birth or baptism. Spon: Wilhelm Gräb.

Rahel of Max Bucks, no dates for birth or baptism. Spon: the mother.

Hanna Sophia of Henry Heberly and wife, b. Jun 4. Spon: Joh Philip Rühr and wife.

Johannes of Andreas Schrötly and wife, b. Jan 6, 1800; bapt. Feb, 1800. Spon: Catarina Schrötly.

Elisabeth of Johann Bretz and wife, b. Oct 1; bapt. Dec, 1800. Spon: parents.

Johannes of Abraham Kopp and wife, b. Oct 6; bapt. Dec, 1800. Spon: Jacob Buchs and wife.

Elisabeth of Philip Fischborn and wife, b. Dec 11; bapt. Apr 11. Spon: parents.

David of Jacob Kamp and wife, b. Oct 29; bapt. Apr 11, 1800. Spon: parents.

Elisabeth of Friedrich Schlotterbeck and wife, no dates for birth or baptism. Spon: Andreas Schrötly and wife.

Johannes of Michael Schäfer and wife, b. May 14; bapt. Jun, 1800. Spon: Dennis Stahl and wife.

Susanna of Christian Kämerer, b. Apr 25. Spon: parents.

David of Johan Hummel and wife, b. May 6. Spon: Anthony Blessly.

Simon of Simon Senger, b. Aug, 1800. Spon: mother.

Wilhelm of Johan Spang, b. Aug, 1800. Spon: Wilhelm Gräb and wife.

Catarina of Adam Kubbach and wife, b. no date. Spon: Wilhelm Gräb.

Johannes of Abraham Kobbach and wife, b. Aug 22, 1800; bapt. Aug,

1800. Spon: Martin Hacker and wife.

Jacob of Georg Zeiter and wife, b. May 1, 1800; bapt. Nov 24, 1800. Spon: Jacob Rinehart.

Michael of William Speidel; bapt. Nov 24, 1800.

Georg of Robert Dunbar and wife, b. Oct 16, 1800; bapt. Nov 24, 1800. Spon: mother.

Madlena of Christian Blesl ÿ and wife, b. Oct 5, 1800; bapt. Nov 24, 1800. Spon: Niklaus Senger and wife.

Johannes of Philip Blesly and wife, b. Sep 31, 1800. Spon: Christian Kämerer and wife.

Burials

Catarina Bälin nee Pfeilin, b. Nov 3, 1734; bapt. and confirmed; m. Ludwig Bähl; d. Sep 24, (1795), age 60 years, 10 mo, 2 weeks. Had 9 children, of whom 7 are living.

Peter Bucks of Peter Bucks and Christina, b. May 7, 1730 in Alsace; bapt. and cofirmed; m. Margar., nee Reimelin 1750; d. Apr, 1796, age 66 years less 20 days. Had 10 children, of whom only 6 are alive, viz. 5 sons, and 1 dau., also had 23 grandchildren.

Elisabetha Schlotterbeckin nee Kerberin, b. 1761; bapt. and confirmed; m. 1781 to Henrich Slotterbeck; d. Apr 27, 1797 age 35 years 4 mos. Had 10 children, of whom 7 are living. Sickness was a hemorrhage, with which she was afflicted only 3 days.

Mar. Salome Blessing nee Wackerin of Johannes Wacker and wife, Anna, b. Sep 29, 1718 in Nieren near Pforzheim; bapt. and confirmed; m. 1744 to Anton Blessing, d. Aug 2, 1797, age 78 years 10 mo, 2 days. Had 9 children of whom only 8 are alive, viz. 6 sons and 2 daus. Sickness was consumption with which she was afflicted nearly 4 years.

David Bähl of Ludwig Bähl and wife, Catarina, b. Oct 27, 1775; confirmed; d. Feb 17, 1798 age 22 years 4 mos, less 12 days. Spon: parents. Sickness smallpox.

Hannah Bucks nee Spring, b. Sep 15, 1762; bapt. Sep 23, 1786; md. Conrad Bucks; d. Sep 13, 1799, age 37 years less 3 days. Sickness was childbirth. Had 8 children with him of whom 3 are still alive.

Henrich of John Conrad and wife, Rosin, born 10 days ago. Baptized by the midwife (Hebamme). Illness, 10 days.[no dates given].

St. John's Evangelical Lutheran Church

Hanna of Rudolph Fuchs and wife, Elisabeth, b. Oct 24; bapt. Dec 3, 1780. Spon: Christian Schnug and wife, Catharine.

Catharina of Hen. Umhols and wife; bapt. May 8, 1781. Spon: Johs Boshart and wife, Catharine.

A dau. of Christian Schnug and wife, Philippina, b. Apr 23; bapt. May 3, 1781. Spon: Hen. Wöffel (Wörstel) and wife, Christina.

Christina of Hen. Wöffel (Wörstel) and wife, Christina, b. Dec 15; bapt. Jan 13, 1782. Spon: J. Died. Steinbrecher and wife, Christina.

Johann Adam of J. Died. Steinbrecher and wife, Christina, b. Jan 3; bapt. Mar 6, 1782. Spon: Christ'n Hoffman and Elisabeth Jägerin, single.

Johannes of Mich. Melgear and wife, Margareth, b. Dec 16, 1782; bapt. Jan 17, 1783. Spon: Johannes Matter and wife, Barbara.

Maria Catharina of Mich. Melgear and wife, Margareth, b. Jan 19; bapt. Mar 9, 1782. Spon: Christ. Schnug and wife, Catharine.

Magdalen of Christ'n Schnug and wife, Catharine, b. Mar 28; bapt. Apr 13, 1783. Spon: Hen. Wörffell (Wölstel) and wife, Christina.

Anna Magdalena of Michel Schädel and wife, Maria, b. Mar 22; bapt. Jun 9, 1783. Spon: Christ. Schnug and wife, Cath.

Maria Margareth of Fried. Paul and wife, Salome, b. May 6; bapt. Jul 6. Spon: Maria Magdalena Schott(in), single.

Anna Maria of Michel Melchior and wife, Marg., b. Feb 1; bapt. Apr 12, 1784. Spon: Jac. Weber and wife, An. Maria.

Nathan of John Woodside, single, b. Feb 8; bapt. Jun 6, 1784. Spon: Johs Matter and Cath Schott(in), single.

Johann Daniel of David Hermann and wife, b. Apr ?; bapt. Aug 1. Spon: Christ Schnug and wife, Catharina.

Johannes of Christian Schnug and wife, Catharina, b. Jan 27; bapt. Feb 6, 1785. Spon: Adam Weiss and wife, Margaretha.

Johannes of Hen. Wörffel (Worstel) and wife, Christina, b. Apr 4; bapt. May 5, 1785. Spon: Isaac Heller and wife, Catharina.

Johann Jacob of Philipp Begdel and wife, Magdalena, b. May 31; bapt. Jul 10, 1785. Spon: Isaac Heller and wife, Catharina.

Anna Catharina of Johannes Matter, Jr. and wife, Elisabeth, b. Aug 14; bapt. Sep 4, 1785. Spon: Pet. Schott and Catharina Matter(in), single.

Johann Georg of Adam Weiss and wife, Marg. Elisabeth, b. Jan 7; bapt. Mar 12, 1786. Spon: Sebast. Steinbrecher and wife, Sussana.

Joh. Michael of Mich. Melchior and wife, Marg., b. Feb 21; bapt. Apr 14, 1786. Spon: Mich. Matter and Marg. Schott(in), single.

Catharina of David Hermann and wife, Elisabeth, b. Mar 14; bapt. Apr 17, 1785. Spon: Baltz. Pittermann and wife, Margareth.

Johann Henrich of Mich. Schädel and wife, Maria, b. May 22; bapt.
Jul 16, 1786. Spon: Johannes Matter, Jr. and wife, Elisabeth.
Anna Catharina of Johannes Matter, Jr. and Elisabeth, b. Aug 14;
bapt. Sep 4, 1785. Spon: Pet. Schott and Catharina Matter(in),
single.
Anna Maria of Christoph Jäger and wife, Eva Catharina, b. Jan 22;
bapt. Feb 18, 1787. Spon: Ad Weiss and wife, Marg. Elisabeth.
Barbara of Baltz. Bittermann and wife, Marg., b. Jan 23; bapt. Mar
18, 1787. Spon: parents.
Johann Georg of Jacob Hofmann and wife, Catharina, b. Mar 1; bapt.
Apr 22, 1787. Spon: Johs Sallentin and wife.
Hanna of Jacob Schmidt and wife, An. Maria, b. Nov 14, 1786; bapt.
Apr 22, 1787. Spon: parents.
Johannes of Johs Jäger and wife, Sussanna, b. Apr 2; bapt. Apr 22,
1787. Spon: Mich. Enderlein and wife, Elisabeth.
Michael of Michel Haak and wife, Catharina, b. Mar 20; bapt. May 21,
1789. Spon: Mich. Sallentin and wife, Christina.
Elisabeth of Johannes Matter, Jr. and wife, Elisabeth, b. ? 24; bapt.
May 28, 1787. Spon: Johannes Matter, Sr. and wife, Catharin.
Elisabeth of Henrich Wörffel (Wörstel) and wife, Christina, b. ? 1;
bapt. May 21, 1787. Spon: Mich. Enderline and wife, Elisabeth.
Elisabeth of Joh. Diedrich Steinbrecher and wife, Christin, b. May 10;
bapt. Jul 15, 1787. Spon: Frid. Häckert and Elisab. Enderlein,
single.
Maria Catharina of Georg Bägdel and wife, An. Maria, b. Jun 17;
bapt. Jul 15. Spon: Bergard Bägdel and wife.
Johann Jacob of Johannes Jäger and wife, Sussana, b. Mar 30; bapt.
Apr 26, 1789. Spon: Isaac Heller and wife, Catharina.
Johann Benjamin of Adam Bänder and wife, Barbara, b. Jun 9; bapt.
Aug 12, 1787. Spon: George Nägely and Marg. Schott(in), single.
Elisabeth of Joseph Paul and wife, Maria, b. Sep 2; bapt. Oct 7, 1787.
Spon: Johs Matter, Jr. and wife, Elisabeth.
Johann Peter of Jacob Schott and wife, Marg., b. Aug 22; bapt. Oct 7,
1787. Spon: Johann Matter and wife, Elisabeth.
Anna Maria of G. Mich. Haak and wife, Catharina, b. Aug 16; bapt.
Oct 7, 1787. Spon: Casp. Emerich and wife, Christina.
Samuel of Leonhard Schneider and wife, Catharina, b. Aug 4; bapt.
Oct 7, 1787. Spon: parents.
Christina Dorothea of Hen. Wolf and wife, Eva, b. Jan 29; bapt. Nov
4, 1787. Spon: Mich. Sallentin and wife, Christ. Doroth.
Anna Catharina of Matth. Deubler and wife, Catharina, b. May 16;

bapt. Jun 1, 1787. Spon: Magd. Haak(in), single.

Johannes of Georg Deubler and wife, Elisabeth, b. Sep 27; bapt. Nov 25. Spon: Johannes Deibler and A. Maria Enderlein, single.

Johann Jacob of Michel Melchior and wife, Margareth, b. Dec 12, 1787; bapt. Mar 9, 1788. Spon: Jon. Weber and wife, An. Maria.

Sussana of Jonathan Miller and wife, Anna, b. Jan 1; bapt. Mar 25, 1788. Spon: Mich. Dieder and wife.

Johann Christoph of Johannes Jäger and wife, Sussanna, b. ? 13; bapt. Mar 23. Spon: Christoph Jäger and wife, Eva Cath.

Sussanna of Ludwig Schitz and wife, Elisabeth, b. Dec 24, 1787; bapt. Apr 20, 1788. Spon: Joh. Nic. Hofman and wife, An. Marg.

Anna Catharina of Georg Paul and wife, Catharina, b. Apr 14; bapt. May 1, 1788. Spon: Johannes Matter, Sr. and wife, A. Catharina.

Johan Adam of Leonh. Kirstetter and wife, Christina, b. Mar 8; bapt. May 18, 1788. Spon: J. Adam Lencker, single.

Johannes of Michael Enderlein and wife, Elisabeth, b. Apr 28; bapt. Jun 15, 1788. Spon: J. Diedrich Steinbrecher and wife, Christina.

Johannes of Michael Matter and wife, A. Maria, b. ? 14; bapt. Jul 20, 1788. Spon: Johannes Matter, Sr., and wife, A. Catharina.

Sussanna Elisabeth of Michael Enderlein and wife, Elisabeth, b. Aug 20; bapt. Sep 13, 1789. Spon: Elisabeth Enderlein, single.

Johannes of Adam Lencker and wife, A. Maria, b. Aug 14; bapt. Oct 11, 1789. Spon: Johann Paul Enderlein, single.

Johannes of Fridrich Paul and wife, Salome, b. Jan 9; bapt. Oct 11, 1789. Spon: Laz. Wengert and Barb. Boshart(in), single.

Sussanna of Henrich Wörffel (Wöstel) and wife, Christina, b. Sep 14; bapt. Nov 15, 1789. Spon: John Nic. Hofmann and wife, Margareth.

Johannes of Georg Paul and wife, Catharina, b. Oct 3; bapt. Nov 15, 1789. Spon: Johannes Matter, Jr. and wife, Elisabeth.

Anna Maria of Jonathan Miller and wife, Anna, b. Oct 20; bapt. Dec 20, 1789. Spon: Jac. Wulandy and wife, Maria Magdalena.

Anna Maria of Michel Matter and wife, An. Maria, b. Jan 21; bapt. Feb 14, 1790. Spon: Joseph Paul and wife, A. Maria.

Christina of Christian Hofmann and wife, Sussanna, b. Dec 25, 1789; bapt. Feb 14, 1790. Spon: Elisabeth Kissinger(in), single.

Johann Jacob of Johannes Matter, Jr. and wife, Elisabeth, b. Feb 7; bapt. Mar 14. Spon: J. Jacob Matter and Elisabeth Enderlein, single.

Johannes of Martin Lubold and wife, Catharina, b. Jun 6; bapt. Aug 29, 1790. Spon: Johannes Hofman and wife, A. Maria.

Sussanna of Georg Boffington and wife, Barbara, b. Aug 25; bapt. Oct 31, 1790. Spon: Michael Enderlein and wife, Elisabeth.

Johann Jacob of Georg Paul and wife, Catharina, b. Mar 6; bapt. Apr 3, 1790. Spon: J. Jac. Matter and Elisabeth Enderlein.

Johann Michael of Michael Matter and An. Maria, b. Mar 29; bapt. Apr 25, 1790. Spon: Michael Enderlein and Elisabeth.

Eva Dorothea of Hen. Wolf and wife, Dorthea, b. Oct 7, 1789; bapt. Dec, 1790. Spon: Mich. Sallentin and wife, Christ. Dorthea.

Michael of Georg Fertig and wife, Magdalen, b. Dec 2; bapt. Dec 28, 1790. Spon: Mich. Sallentin and wife, Christ. Dorothea.

Elisabeth of Math. Deibler and wife, Catharina, b. Apr 22; bapt. May 1, 1791. Spon: Elisabeth Eschweiler.

Johannes of Johannes Matter and wife, Elisabeth, b. Sep 30; bapt. Oct 12, 1788. Spon: Joseph Paul and wife, An. Maria.

Elisabeth of Dav. Herman and wife, Elisabeth, b. Aug 10; bapt. Oct 12, 1788. Spon: J. David Grob and wife, Elisabeth.

Elisabeth of Christoph Jäger and wife, Eva Catharina, b. Aug 4; bapt. Oct 12, 1788. Spon: Philipp Bägdell and wife, M. Catharin.

Elisabeth of Philipp Bägdel and wife, M. Catharina, b. ? 6; bapt. Dec 25, 1788. Spon: Christoph Jäger and wife, Eva Catharin.

Johann Jacob of Johannes Hofmann and wife, An. Maria, b. Jan 28, 1789; bapt. Apr 5, 1789. Spon: Christian Hofmann and wife, Sussanna.

Anna Maria of Joseph Paul and wife, An. Maria, b. Jun 1; bapt. Jul 19, 1789. Spon: Michael Matter and wife, A. Maria.

Johann Philipp of Jacob Schott and wife, Margareth, b. Aug 5; bapt. the Sep 13, 1789. Spon: Johannes Matter and wife, Elisabeth.

Jacob of Baltzer Bitterman (Pittermann) and wife, Margareth, b. Apr 12; bapt. Sep 13. Spon: parents.

David of Joseph Paul and wife, Anna Maria, b. Apr 19; bapt. May 29, 1791. Spon: Mich. Matter and wife, A. Maria.

Johannes of Philipp Bägdell and wife, Catharina, b. ? 5; bapt. Aug 21, 1791. Spon: Christoph Jäger and wife, Eva Cath.

Jonas of David Herman and wife, Elisabeth, b. Jul 3; bapt. Aug 21, 1791. Spon: Baltz. Pittermann and wife, A. Margareth.

Wilhelm of Michael Enderlein and wife, Elisabeth, b. Sep 22; bapt. Nov 13, 1791. Spon: Adam Lencker and wife, A. Maria.

Elisabeth of Christian Hofmann and wife, Susanna, b. Nov 8; bapt. Dec 11, 1791. Spon: Christina Deiblerler(in).

Philipp of J. Georg Brosius and wife, Suss, b. Oct 5; bapt. Dec 8, 1791. Spon: Philipp Haak and wife, Juliana Popp(in).

Johann Jacob of Henrich Wörffel (Worstel) and wife, Christina, b. Sep 20, 1791; bapt. Mar 4, 1792. Spon: Jac. Herman and wife, Marg.

Elisabeth of Pet. Schnock and wife, Marg, b. Nov 16, 1791; bapt. Apr 1, 1792. Spon: Elisab Peter(in).

Johann Michael of Adam Lencker and wife, An. Maria, b. Feb 6; bapt. Apr 1. Spon: Phil. Lencker and wife, Elisabeth.

Anna Margareth of Baltzer Bittermann (Pitterman) and wife, Marg., b. Mar 15; bapt. Apr 29, 1792. Spon: Jac. Herman and wife, Margareth.

Johann Borckhard of Joh. Georg Begdel and wife, An. Maria, b. Mar 14; bapt. May 27, 1792. Spon: Jacob Dieder.

Johann Christian of Johannes Matter and wife, Elisabeth, b. ? 8; bapt. Jul 22, 1792. Spon: Christian Schott and wife, Barbara. Matter(in), single.

Isaac of Georg Paul and wife, Catharina, b. Jul 6; bapt. Aug 26, 1792. Spon: Isaac Heller and wife, Catharina.

Johann Georg of Michael Matter and wife, An. Maria, b. ? 16; bapt. Mar 10, 1793. Spon: Georg Matter and wife, Catharina.

Sussanna of Matth. Deibler and wife, Catharina, b. Dec 12, 1792; bapt. Mar 10, 1793. Spon: Johannes Bortner and wife, Sussanna.

Andreas of Johannes Jäger and wife, Suss., b. Jan 15; bapt. Apr 1, 1793. Spon: Jac. Welandy and wife.

Maria Elisabeth of Michael Enderlein and wife, Mar. Elis., b. Feb 4; bapt. Mar 26, 1793. Spon: Maria Heller.

Hanna of Valantin Sommerlade and wife, An. Elisabeth, b. Jan 10; bapt. May 5, 1793. Spon: parents.

Johann Georg of Johs Jäger and wife, Sussanna, b. Aug 30; bapt. Oct 4, 1795. Spon: Christian Schnug and wife, Margaretha Jäger(in).

Johannes of Georg Matter and wife, Catharina, b. Oct 25; bapt. ? 6, 1795. Spon: Joh. Matter Sr. and wife, Catharina.

Peter of Joh. Paul Enderlein and wife, Charlotta, b. Dec 11; bapt. Dec 25, 1795. Spon: Mich. Enderlein and wife, Elisabeth.

Peter of Geor. Lerg (Berg?) and wife, Anna Catharina, b. Nov, 20; bapt. Dec 20, 1795. Spon: Stephan Lencker and wife, Sussanna.

Magdalena of Jacob Lencker and wife, Elisabeth, b. Aug 14; bapt. Dec 20, 1795. Spon: Georg Lerg (Berg) and wife, Elisabeth.

Johann Philipp of Stephan Lencker and wife, Sussanna, b. Aug 12; bapt. Dec 20, 1795. Spon: Philipp Lencker and wife, Elisabeth.

Jacob of Adam Lencker and wife, An. Maria, b. Feb 10; bapt. Feb 22, 1795. Spon: Jacob Schäfer and wife, Margareth.

Johann Matteis of J. Georg Brosius and wife, Sussanna, b. Sep 12, 1795; bapt. Jan 3, 1796. Spon: Mattheis Haak.

Johann Adam of Joh. Adam Matter and wife, Margareth, b. Jul 4, 1796; bapt. Jan 24. Spon: Jacob Matter and wife, Catharina.

Jonas of Georg Paul and wife, Catharina, b. 1796; bapt. Oct 25, 1796. Spon: Mich. Matter and wife, Anna Maria.

Margareth of Michael Radel and wife, Margareth, b. 1796; bapt. Oct 25, 1796. Spon: Adam Weiss and wife, Margareth.

Philip of Michael Enderlein and wife, Elisabeth, b. Sep 30, 1796; bapt. Nov 13, 1796. Spon: John Paul Enderlein and wife, Charlotta.

Catharina of Johannes Salentin and Elisabeth Hofmann(in), not wed, b. May 14; bapt. Aug 14, 1796. Spon: Philipp Klinger and wife, Catharina.

Sara of Johann P. Enderlein and wife, Charlotta, b. Dec 24, 1796; bapt. Jan 15, 1797. Spon: Johannes Matter and wife, Elisabeth.

Maria Magdalena of Jacob Matter and wife, Catharina, b. Nov 20, 1796, bapt. Jan 8, 1797. Spon: Maria Magdalena Weber(in) and J. Adam Heller, single.

Henrich of Michael Matter and wife, An. Maria, b. Dec 26, 1796; bapt. Jan 29, 1797. Spon: Henrich Ramberger and wife, Elisabeth.

Maria Margaretha of J. Adam Liepoh and wife, Catharina, b. Dec 12, 1796; bapt. Jan 29, 1797. Spon: Samuel Bayer and wife, Maria Margaret.

Johan Adams of J. Peter Metz and wife, Charlotta, b. ?, 7; bapt. Feb 9, 1797. Spon: Sebastian Metz and wife, Catharina.

Elisabeth of J. Georg Schneider and wife, Gerthraut, b. ? 1; bapt. Feb 9, 1797. Spon: Elisabeth Neuman(in), widow.

Maria Sussanna of Mattheus Haak and wife, Sussanna, b. Feb 17; bapt. Mar 26, 1797. Spon: Philipp Haak and wife, Barb Deibler(in).

Johann Georg of Jacob Brosius and wife, Christina, b. Jan 19; bapt. Apr 6, 1797. Spon: J. Georg Brosius and wife, Sussanna.

Maria Sarah of Leonh. Kirstetter and wife, Christina, b. Nov 30, 1796; bapt. May 25, 1797. Spon: Jac. Jäckel and wife; Mar. Sarah Hahn(in), single.

Maria Magdalena of Joseph Paul and wife, An. Maria, b. Nov 31, 1796; bapt. May 25, 1797. Spon: Matthias Weimar and wife, Magdalena.

Joseph of Georg Matter and wife, Catharina b. May 16, 1797; bapt. May 21, 1797. Spon: Balthaser Ramberger.

Emanuel of Johannes Diederich and wife, A. Barbara, b. Jun 24; bapt.

Aug 2, 1797. Spon: John Matter, Grandfather.

Samuel of Henrich Wittmer and wife, Catharina, b. Aug 12, 1797; bapt. Aug 8, 1797. Spon: Stepan Laah (Lash) and wife, Marg.

Elisabeth of Carl Coleman and wife, Barbara, b. Sep 3, 1797; bapt. same day. Spon: C. Elis. Bosshart(in).

Anna Chadarina of Michael Matter and wife, An. Maria, b. Feb 14, 1798; bapt. Mar 25, 1798. Spon: Georg Matter and wife, Chadarina.

Catharina of Adam Ramberger and wife, A. Maria, b. Sep 2; bapt. Oct 29. Spon: Baltzer Ramberger and wife, Susanna.

C. Magdalena of Johannes Sambre and wife, Barbara, b. St. John's Day; bapt. the same day. Spon: Hartmann Rickert and wife, Magdalena.

Eva Maria of Johannes Sambre and wife, Barbara, b. Oct 10, 1796; bapt. same day. Spon: Eva Maria Sambre.

Georg of Georg Matter and wife, Catharina, b. Oct 11; bapt. same day. Spon: Georg Holtzmann and wife, Elisabeth.

Margaretha of Johann Adam Matter and wife, Margaretha, b. Oct 14; bapt. same day. Spon: Johannes Matter and wife, Salome.

Johann Georg of Joh. Georg Brosius and wife, Sussanna, b. Dec 6, 1797 bapt. ? 13, 1797. Spon: Georg Daniel Brosius and wife, Elisabeth.

Barbara of John M'Kenny and wife, Mary, b. Feb 16, 1797; bapt. Jul 9, 1797. Spon: Isaac Heller and wife, Catharina.

Magdalena of Jacob Dieter and wife, Magdalena, b. Jan 23, 1797; bapt. Dec 31, 1797. Spon: parents.

Sussanna of Johannes Matter Jr., and wife, Elisabeth, b. Jan 26, 1798; bapt. Mar 18, 1798. Spon: Mich. Enderlein and wife, Elisabeth.

Balthaser of Jacob Matter and wife, Catharina, b. Mar 8, 1798; bapt. Apr 21, 1798. Spon: Balthaser Bitterman (Pittermann) and wife, An. Margareth.

Magdalena of Peter Schott and wife, Magdalena, b. Feb 28, 1798; bapt. May 21, 1798. Spon: Lud. Schott and wife, Catharina.

Anna Maria of Joh. Paul Enderlein and wife, Charlotta, b. Apr 13, 1798; bapt. Jun 5, 1798. Spon: parents.

Johannes of Samuel Ludwig and wife, Mar. Catharina, b. May 31, 1798; bapt. Jul 8, 1798. Spon: Adam Bender and wife, Barbara.

Johannes of Joh. Adam Herrman and wife, b. Oct 15, 1798; bapt. Jan 20, 1799. Spon: Joh Jacob Schott and Maria Elisabeth Schott(in), single.

Maria Magdalena of Jac. Alleman and wife, Elisabeth, b. Jan 7, 1799; bapt. Feb 3, 1799. Spon: Magdalena Emmerich, single.

Georg of John Michael Enderlein and wife, Elisabeth, b. Jan 4, 1799; bapt. Mar 24, 1799. Spon: Adam Kupper and wife, Christina.

Johannes of Georg Schneider and wife, Catharina, b. Aug 10, 1798; bapt. May 5, 1799. Spon: Joh. Messner and Margareth Bender, single.

A. Maria of Andreas Daniel and wife, Susanna, b. Sep 15, 1798; bapt. May 26, 1799. Spon: Jakob Schneider and wife, Catharina.

Jakob of Jakob Jackel and wife, A. Maria, b. Mar 17; bapt. May 26, 1799. Spon: Heinrich Hehn (Lehr) and wife, Maria Sara.

Susanna of Peter Ritzmann and wife, Cath. Elisabeth, b. Feb 27, 1799; bapt. May 26, 1799. Spon: Jakob Salade and wife, Susanna.

Juliana of Mattheus Haag and wife, Susanna, b. Jan 23; bapt. May 26, 1799. Spon: Willhelm Bartmann and wife, Elisabeth.

Anna of Mattheus Grönewald and wife, A. Maria, b. Apr 20; bapt. May 26, 1799. Spon: Georg Puffentaun and wife, Barbara.

J. Georg of Georg Paul and wife, A. Cath. b. Dec 5; bapt. May 26, 1799. Spon: Georg Matter and wife, Catharina.

Johannes of Joh. Diederich and wife, A. Barbara, b. Nov 26; bapt. May 26, 1799. Spon: Johannes Matter and wife, Elizabeth.

Johanne of Philip Haag and wife, Cath. b. Mar 25; bapt. May 26, 1799. Spon: J. Died. Steinbrecher and wife, Christina.

Susanna of Peter Willert and wife, Catharina, b. Feb 24; bapt. May 26, 1799. Spon: Susanna Willet.

Michael of Henrich Wolf and wife, Eva, b. Mar 6; bapt. May 26, 1799. Spon: Michael Salade and wife, Christina.

A. Catharina of Georg Hermann and wife, Catharina, b. Jun 9; bapt. Jul 7, 1799. Spon: Jakob Hermann and wife, A. Catharina.

Regina of Henrich Schafstall and wife, Elisabeth, b. Sep 7, 1798; bapt. Jul 7, 1799. Spon: Cath. Schneider(in).

Susanna of Balthasar Ramberger and wife, Susanna, b. Apr 16; bapt. Jul 7, 1799. Spon: Andreas Daniel and wife, Susanna.

Johannes of Adam Wolf and wife, Christina, b. May 26; bapt. Jul 7, 1799. Spon: Adam Bär and wife, Susanna.

Elisabeth of Henrich Ramberger and wife, Elisabeth, b. Dec 14, 1798; bapt. Jul 7, 1799. Spon: Elisabeth Hoffmänn(in).

Elisabeth of Michael Matter and wife, A. Maria, b. May 16; bapt. Jul 7, 1799. Spon: Johannes Matter and wife, Elisabeth.

Catharina of Peter Portner and wife, Magdalena (Catharina?), b. Jul 7. Spon: Peter Imschafstall and wife, Catharina.

Jakob of Johannes Imschafstall and wife, Magdalena, b. Mar (July ?) 16. Spon: Peter Imschafstall and wife, Catharina.

Rahel of Jakob Hermann, Jr. and wife, Magdalena, b. Jul 17. Spon: Jakob Herman, Sr. and wife, Margaretha.

Jakob of Johannes Harrmann and wife, Anna Maria, b. Sep 30, 1799; bapt. Nov 10. Spon: Adam Weiss and wife, Marg. Elisabeth.

Maria of David Wolf and wife, Cath., b. Sep 18; bapt. Nov 10. Spon: Adam Bär and wife, Susanna.

Joh. Jakob of Georg Holtzmann and wife, Elis., b. Sep 23; bapt. Nov 10. Spon: Joh. Jäger and wife, Cath.

Elisabeth of Martin Paul and wife, Elisabeth, b. Apr 13, 1796; bapt. May 11, 1800. Spon: Mattheus Weimert and wife, Magdalena.

Sophia of Martin Paul and wife, Elisabeth, b. Feb 20, 1799; bapt. May 11, 1800. Spon: Philip Haman and wife, Margaretha.

Anna and Johannes, twins, of Jonathan Müller and wife, A. Maria, b. Jan 30, 1800; bapt. May 11, 1800. Spon: Catharina Schneider and Fried. Lupold and wife Elisab.

Salome of Joseph Paul and wife, Maria, b. Oct 4, 1799; bapt. May 11, 1800. Spon: Johannes Marter, Sr. and wife, Salome.

Daniel of Fried. Etzweiler and wife, Catharina, b. Apr 9, 1800; bapt. May 11, 1800. Spon: Adam Wolf and wife, Christina.

A. Catharina of Joh. Adam Schrayer and wife, Maria Elisabeth, b. Jan 27, 1800; bapt. May 11, 1800. Spon: A. Cath. Brosius.

Adam of Peter Hehn and wife, Cath. b. Apr 20, 1800; bapt. May 11, 1800. Spon: Henrich Hehn and wife, Maria Sara.

Amalia of Jakob Diederich and wife, A. Magdalena, b. Feb 14, 1799; bapt. May 11, 1800. Spon: parents.

Philip of Philip Hoock (Haak?) and wife, Charlotta, b. Jan 22, 1800; bapt. May 11, 1800. Spon: Richard Hartmann.

Joseph of Michael Redel and wife, A. Margaretha, b. Dec 1, 1799; bapt. May 11, 1800. Spon: Joseph Wirth and wife, Barbara.

Elisabeth of Johann Paul Enderlein and Charlotta, b. May 15, 1799; bapt. May 11, 1800. Spon: Johannes Moor and wife, Philippina.

Susanna of Johann Paul Enderlein and Charlotta, b. Jun 18; bapt. Jul 13, 1800. Spon: Susanna Heller(in).

Johannes of Johannes Salade and wife, A. Maria, b. 3 weeks 4 days old, 1800; bapt. Jul 13, 1800. Spon: Johannes Kissinger.

Elisabeth of Adam Lenkert and wife, A. Maria, b. May 28, 1800; bapt. Jul 13, 1800. Spon: Daniel Wolf and Elis. Spät.

Willhelm of Jacob Schwab and wife, A. Maria, b. Jul 27, 1800; bapt. Aug 8, 1800. Spon: Willhelm Portner and wife, Elisabeth.

Maria Sarah of Johannes Diederich and wife, A. Barbara, b. May 23, 1800; bapt. Sep 7. Spon: Maria Sarah Diedeich(in).

Peter of Peter Bellos and wife, Elisabeth, b. Jul 13, 1799; bapt. Sep 7, 1800. Spon: Christian Hofmann and wife, Susanna.

A. Rosina of Jakob Lenkert and wife, A. Cath. b. last Jun; bapt. Sep 7, 1800. Spon: Anthony Docky (Dail?) and wife, Anna Rosina.

Joseph of Henrich Bellos and wife, Margaretha, b. May 25; Sep 7, 1800. Spon: Joh. Bellos and wife, Catharina.

Michael of Georg Schatel and Susanna, b. Sep 9, 1800; bapt. Oct 1, 1800. Spon: Michael Schetel and M. Cadarina.

Daniel of Jakob Martter and wife, Catharina, b. Sep 25, 1800; bapt. Nov 2, 1800. Spon: Joh. Martter and wife, Elisabeth.

A. Catharina of Michael Martter and wife, A. Maria, b. Oct 7; bapt. Nov 2, 1800. Spon: Georg Martter and wife, A. Catharina.

Magdalena of Hartmann Rickert and wife, Catharina, b. Aug 24, 1800; bapt. Nov 2, 1800. Spon: Friedrich Lupold and wife, Elisabeth.

Peter of Peter Weber and wife, Catharina, b. May 10; bapt. Nov 2, 1800. Spon: Peter Leppo and wife, Catharina.

Joh. Georg of Joh. Philip Haag and wife, Catharina, b. Dec 8, 1800; bapt. same day. Spon: Joh. Ad. Steinbrecher.

Joh. Philip of Johannes Rädel and wife, Susanna, b. Sep 10, 1800; Apr 26, 1801. Spon: Joh. Philip Schryer and wife, Catharina.

Susanna of Joh. Belless and wife, Catharina, b. Sep 15, 1800; bapt. Jun 21, 1801. Spon: Jacob Runck and wife, Catharina.

BADELL, Philipp, 83
BAECKER,
  Elizabeth, 4
BAEDER, Elizabeth,
  10
  Henry, 5, 10
  Margaret, 5, 10
  Susanna, 5
BAGDEL, An. Maria,
  81
  Bergard, 81
  Georg, 81
  Maria Catharina,
  81
BAGDELL,
  Elisabeth, 83
  Johannes, 83
  M. Catharin, 83
  M. Catharina, 83
BAHL, Catarina, 79
  David, 79
  Ludwig, 79
BAHNA, Elisabeth,
  35
BAHNER, Johannes,
  43
  Margretha, 43
  Nicolaus, 43
BAHR, Adam, 45, 46
  Johannes, 45
  Susanna, 45, 46
BAKER, Christian,
  64
  Elisabeth, 64
  Jacob, 64
  Mary, 59
BALDLY, Henry, 8
  John, 8
  Margaret, 8
BALIN, Catarina, 79

BALLES, Catharina,
  48
  Joh., 48
  Magdalena, 48
BANDER, Adam, 81
  Barbara, 81
  Johann Benjamin,
  81
BANDON, Elizabeth,
  3
  Mansfield, 3
  William, 3
BANDSTETTER,
  Anna Barbara, 39
  Fridrich, 39
BAR, Adam, 47, 88
  Susanna, 47, 88
BARDEMER,
  Catarina, 74
  Johannes, 74
BAROFF, Adam, 19
  Barbara, 19
  Maria Dora, 19
BARTHOLOME,
  Michel, 25
BARTHOMER, Eva,
  37
  Philip, 37
BARTMANN,
  Elisabeth, 87
  Willhelm, 87
BASLER, Catherine,
  8
BATER, Cath., 31
  Christ, 31
BAUER, Georg, 73
  Michael, 54, 65
  Rosina, 73
  Vernonica, 54
  Veronica, 65

BAUERMAN,
  Catharina, 66
BAUM, Catharina,
  16
  Johannes, 16
BAUMANN, Georg
  Jacob, 69
  Jacob, 69
BAUMANN
  (BOWMAN),
  Henrich, 64
  Margareth, 64
BAUMGARTNER,
  Elisabeth, 15
  Heinrich, 15
  Jacob, 15
BAYER, Anna, 8
  Catharin, 64
  Catharine, 28
  Christian, 28, 33
  Christina, 33
  Elisabeth, 30
  Elizabeth, 24
  Ephraim, 8
  Eva Margretha, 45
  Jacob, 8
  Johannes, 64
  John Peter, 13
  Jonathan, 24
  Margaret, 9, 10
  Maria Margaret, 85
  Peter, 9, 10
  Philip, 30
  Samuel, 30, 45, 85
BEATTY, Mary
  Brereton, 61
  Nancy, 60
BECHTEL, Anna
  Maria, 48
  Barbara, 27

Baltzer, 84
Marg., 84
BITTNER, Mr., 58
BLASSER, Christian, 13
BLEIMEIR, John, 2
Lydia, 2
BLESLY, Christian, 75, 76, 78, 79
Friedrich, 76
Johannes, 79
Madlena, 79
Philip, 76, 79
Sara, 78
BLESSING, Anna Margaretha, 73
Anthony, 77
Anton, 79
Antony, 73
Catar., 77
Catharina, 73
Christian, 77
Fridrich, 16
Joannes, 73
Johannes, 77
Mar. Salome, 79
Philip, 77
BLESSLE, Antoni, 72
Antonius, 70, 71
Antoniy, 73
Antonj, 69, 70
Antony, 72
Christian, 70
Georg Fridrich, 70
Magdalena, 72
Philipp, 72
Salome, 72
BLESSLY, Anthony, 78

Catharine, 17
Michael, 78
Philip, 78
BLISS, Philip, 68
BOAL, Robert, 58
BOBB, Barbara, 17, 20, 22
Catharine, 19
Conrad, 17
Elizabeth, 21
Eva, 17
Gertrude, 20, 21, 22
John, 18
John George, 17
John Jacob, 21
Peter, 17, 20, 21
Philip, 20, 21, 22
BOCKS, Johan Peter, 75
BODAMER, Anna Eva, 37
Cathrina, 38
Joh. Phil., 37
Johan, 38
Johan Jacob, 37
Mary Elizabeth, 38
BODEN, David, 77
BODENSTEIN, Catarina, 77
Christr., 77
Elisab., 77
Philip, 77
BOFFENDEN, Georg, 45
BOFFENTON, Barbara, 46
Elias., 35
Elisabeth, 35
Georg, 46

Johannes, 35
BOFFINGTON, Barbara, 43, 83
Elias., 33
Elisabeth, 33
Georg, 43, 83
Maria Catharina, 33
Rahel, 43
BOFINGTON, Barbara, 41, 42, 45, 46
Elisabetha, 41
Georg, 41, 42, 45, 46
Isaac, 42
Levi, 45
Solomon, 45
Susanna, 45
Susanna Catharina, 46
BOHL, Anna Maria, 1
Elizabeth, 1
Henry, 1
John, 1
Margaret, 1
Rebecca, 1
BOHM, Barbara, 16
Christian, 16
Maria, 16
BOHNER, Cath., 29, 32, 33, 34
Catharina, 29
Friederich, 27
Hen., 34
Henr., 32
Henrich, 29, 33
Johan Henrich, 34
Mar. Margreth, 29

Johannes, 68
John, 66
Joseph, 52
Magdalena, 64, 66
Maria, 14
Melchior, 14
Philip, 7
Sarah, 64
Susanna, 13, 56
Vincenz, 68
BRECHTBILL,
  Dorothy, 23
John George, 23
BREININGER, John
  Peter, 1
Margaret, 1
Wendel, 1
BREIS, Gertrude, 5
BRENNER, John, 7
Magdalene, 7
BRETZ, Anna Maria,
  53
Catharina, 15
Elisabeth, 15, 78
Johann, 78
Johannes, 15, 77
Magdalena, 16
Wilhelm, 15
BRETZIN, Andon,
  74
Susanna, 74
BREZ, Simon, 69
BRICE, Alexander,
  58
BRISBAN,
  Margaret, 62
BROISUS,
  Elisabeth, 86
Georg Daniel, 86
Joh. Georg, 86

Johann Georg, 86
Susanna, 86
BROSIUS, A. Cath.,
  88
A. Maria, 27, 30
Abraham, 27, 28,
  29, 30, 32
An. Maria, 32
Cath., 27, 29, 30
Catharina, 27, 30
Catharine, 28
Christina, 85
George, 27
J. Georg, 84, 86
J. Goerge, 85
Jacob, 85
Jo. George, 30
Jo. Nicholaus, 29
Jo. Nicolaus, 30
Joh. George, 27, 30
Joh. Nice., 27
Joh. Nicholaus, 27
Johan Jacob, 27
Johann, 32
Johann Georg, 85
Johann Matteis, 85
John. Nicholaus, 27
M. Cath., 32
M. Catharina, 29
Maria, 27, 29
Maria Elisabth, 29
Mary, 27
Philipp, 84
Suss, 84
Sussanna, 85, 86
BROUCH, Felton,
  39
Susannah Marg.,
  39
BROUCHIN, Anna

Eva, 39
BROWN, Dina, 38
Elisabeth, 18
James, 58
Magdalena, 51
Mary, 38
Sarah, 59
Thomas, 38
William, 58
BRUNDLE,
  Cathrina, 39, 40
Ferena, 39
Johan Melchoir, 39
Johannes, 39
John, 39, 40
Lorenz, 39
BRUNNER,
  Catherine, 14
Elizabeth, 10
Henry, 1, 3, 10, 14
John Jacob, 10
Juliana Charlotte, 1
Maria Eva, 3
Susanna, 1, 3, 10
BRUNSON,
  Barefoot, 58
BUCHER, Elizabeth,
  5, 8, 24
George, 5, 8, 12
Jacob, 6, 10, 24
John, 24
John Conrad, 6
John George, 5
Maria Elizabeth, 10
Susanna, 6, 10
BUCHS, Anna
  Margaretha, 73
Elisab., 74
Elisabetha, 73
Jacob, 74, 78

CARSON, Elizabeth,
63
James, 58
CASSEEL, J., 66
CASSEL, Anna
Catharina, 69
Catharina, 64
Catherine, 9
Christian, 21
Christiana, 20
Esther, 21
Frederick, 18, 20,
21
Fridrich, 69, 71, 72
Georg Fridrcih, 71
George, 9
Joann, 71, 73
Joann Michael, 69
Joannes, 71
Ludwig, 64
Maria Eva, 72
Maria Magdalena,
72
Michael, 69, 72
Nicobus, 71
Sabina, 9
CATCH, James, 38
Susannah, 38
CATHCART, Sarah,
60
CAVET, James, 58
CEHLER, Antony,
71
CHAMBERS,
Benjamin, 58
Margaret, 58
Maxwell, 58
CHESNEY, John, 58
CHRISTY, William,
58

CLARK, Charles, 58
John, 58
William, 58
CLAUER, Anna
Maria, 5
Elizabeth, 5, 7
Jacob, 7
Jonathan, 5
COCHRAN, Anna,
59
Martha, 61
COLEMAN,
Barbara, 86
Carl, 86
Elisabeth, 86
COLLIER, Susan, 62
COLLMER, Joann
Martin 71
COLMANN,
Hannah, 42
COLMEIN, Hanna,
28
COMFOET, John, 2
Philippina, 2
COMFORT , John, 1
CONRAD, A. Maria,
26
Anna Maria, 25
Annamaria, 25
Elizabeth, 4, 7
Henrich, 80
Henry, 4, 7
John, 25, 80
John Jacob, 25
John Nicholas, 25
Maria, 26
Maria Margaret, 25
Nicholas, 26
Rosin, 80
COOK, Wiliam, 58

COWDEN,
Elizabeth, 60
James, 58
Mary, 63
COX, Catharine, 59
CRAIN, George, 58
CROUCH, Elizabeth,
59
Mary, 58
CUBERTSON,
James, 58
CURRY, Agnes, 58
Daniel, 58
William, 58

-D-
DANBENBERGER,
Jacob, 76
DANCKMANN,
Michael, 71
DANIEL, A. Maria,
87
Agnes, 73
Andreas, 44, 45, 46,
87, 88
Catharina, 46
Johann, 73
Susanna, 44, 45,
46, 87, 88
DAUBENHEIER,
Andrew, 7
Christine, 7
Peter, 7
DAUBLER, Anna
Catharina, 46
Anna Maria, 46
Mathaeus, 43
Matheis, 46
DAUDIN, Catharina,
74

M. Christina, 32
M. Magdalena, 28
Maria, 36
Philipps, 33
DIETZ, Conrath, 43
Joh. Conrath, 32
Johannes, 32
John, 17
Marg., 32
Margareth, 50
Margretha, 43
DIETZEL, Hennrich,
    71
DINDORF,
    Elizabeth, 9
    Philip, 5
DINGER, Barbara,
    31
Frederich, 32
Fredrich, 31
Jo. Peter, 31
Joh. George, 32
M. Barbara, 32
Peter, 31
DITTY, Anna Maria,
    54
Johanes, 54
Magdalena, 54
Maria, 50
DITZEL, Barbara,
    74
Catharina, 67, 74
Hen., 67
Hennrich, 70, 73,
    74
Henrich, 67
Joann Hennrich, 73
Joann Philipp, 73
Johannes, 74
DIXON, George, 58

Isabella, 61
Sankey, 59
DOBLER, Barbara,
    51
Elisabetha, 51
Matheyss, 51
DOCKY (DAIL),
    Anna Rosina, 89
    Anthony, 89
DOLL, Elizabeth, 12
    John, 12
DONALDSON,
    James, 59
DUBENDORFF,
    Samuel, 55
DUBENTORF, An-
    na, 35
    Friederich, 35
DUBS, Catharina, 51
    Heinrich, 51
DUEN, Susanna, 68
    William, 68
DUGAL, Mr., 59
DUNBAR, Georg, 79
    Joseph, 78
    Magdalena, 15
    Robert, 15, 78, 79
    Sussanna, 15
DUNCAN, Andrew,
    59
DUNCKAH,
    Eleanora, 37
    John, 37
    Margreth, 37
DUNCKEL,
    Elisabeth, 64
    Johannes, 64
    Susanna, 64
DUNKAN,
    Eleanorah, 37

John, 37
DUPENDORF, An-
    na, 43
    Johan Friedrich, 43
    Samuel Tobias, 43
DURANG
    (DURANY), Char.,
    13
    John C., 13
    Mary, 13

-E-
EASTON, John, 14
EBERHARD,
    Elisabetha, 67
    Friedrich, 67
EBERHARDT,
    Margaretha 52
EBERHART,
    Catherine, 5
    Gottfried, 5
    Gottfried (Godfrey)
    5
EBERT, Anna
    Maria, 2
    Elizabeth, 1, 2, 5
    John, 1, 2, 5
    Michael, 1
    Salome, 5
EBRECHT, Hannah,
    3, 6, 9, 10
    Jacob, 3, 6, 9, 10
ECKSTEIN, David,
    16
EDER, Barbara, 34
    Johannes, 34
EGLEE, Maria
    Cath., 12
    Philip, 13
EIDENEIER, Anna

ERNSTIN,
  Catharina, 73
ERVIN, Christina,
  25
  Maria Margaretta,
  25
  William, 25
ESCHWEILER,
  Elisabeth 83
ESHENAUER, John
  Christian, 38
  Leong, 38
  Margreth, 38
ESPY, Mary, 58
ETGEN, Abraham,
  64
  Cathrina, 64
  Elisabeth, 64
  Margreta, 64
  Philipp, 64
ETSCHWEILER,
  Cathar. Elisab., 57
ETTELIN, Catharina
  Elisabeta 70
  Christina, 70
  Conrad, 70
  David, 70
  Gottlieb David, 70
  J. Philipp, 70
ETZWEILER,
  Catharina, 88
  Daniel, 88
  Elisabeth, 44, 54
  Fried., 88
  Georg, 54
  Greth, 50
ETZWEILERIN,
  Anna Maria 68
EWEN, Anna Maria,
  21

Christiana, 21
William, 21
EWIG, Barbara, 2
  Christian, 2
  Christine, 2
EZWEYLER, Cathr.
  Elizab., 40
  George, 40
  Maria, 40

-F-
FABER, Catharine,
  64
  Christine, 8
  Johannes, 64
  William, 8
FACKLER,
  Elizabeth, 9
  George, 8, 9
  John, 9
  Rachael, 20
  Susanna, 8
FAHRLING, Jacob,
  19
  Maria Salome, 19
FARRINGER,
  Christina, 36
  Elisabeth, 35
  George, 36
  Joh. George, 35
  Martin, 35
FEEHSS, Cath., 29
  Henrich, 29
  Jacob, 29
FEESER, Dorothy,
  23
  George, 23
FEHRLING,
  Abraham, 21
  Catharine, 20, 22

Daniel, 20, 21, 22
Jacob, 20, 21, 22
John, 20
Maria Magdalena,
  21
Salome, 20, 21
FEITH, Georg, 55
  Rahel, 55
FELTY, Catharine,
  18
  Christiana, 21
  John, 21
  John Michael, 18
  Peter, 18
FERREE, Mrs., 14
FESSLER, Cathrine,
  7
  Jacob, 7
  John, 7
  Maria, 7
FEY, George, 68
FILTY, Magdalena,
  21
FINDLAY, John, 59
FISBORN, Anna
  Maria, 15
  Jacob, 15
  Philip, 15
FISCHBORININ,
  Elisabeth, 67
  Margaretha, 67
FISCHBORN,
  Antony, 71
  Catharine Elisabeta
  71
  Elisabeth, 78
  Joan Dietrich, 71
  Joann Peter, 71
  Joann Philipp, 71
  Ludwig, 71

Catharine, 17
Elisabeth, 65
Elizabeth, 17, 64
G. Adam, 64
Henrich, 67
John, 17
FROMM, David, 72
Elisabetha, 72
Rosina, 72
FUCHS (FOX),
Anna Maria, 56
Catharina, 56
Catherine, 23
Elisabeth, 80
Frantz, 23
Hanna, 80
Rudolph, 80
FULK, Mary, 60
FULLION, Jean, 61
FULTON, Benjamin,
59
Grizel, 59, 63
Isabella, 63
Jean, 62
Joseph, 59
Richard, 59
FURST, Cath., 27
Henrich, 27

-G-
GALBRAITH,
Benjamin, 59
GALD, Catharine, 24
John, 24
Richard, 24
GALLY, Anna
Caatharina, 42
Maria, 42
Michael, 42
GANSLE, J. Adam,

69
Michael, 69
GARVERICH,
Barbara, 22
John, 22
Maria Elizabeth, 22
GAST, Anna
Margaret, 2
John Matthew, 2
GAUL, Anna Maria,
21, 23
John, 21, 23
Philip, 23
GEHRES, Elisabeth,
36
Jacob, 36
Sara, 36
GEMBERLING,
Carl, 13
Maria, 13
GENSEL, Michael,
68
GENTER, Catarina
Elisabeta 68
Johan Peter, 68
Philipp, 68
GEPHART,
Abraham, 76
Peter, 76
GERBERICH, John,
10
GERBERICK,
George, 24
Hanna, 24
John Jacob, 24
Margaret, 24
Philip, 24
GERESS, An. Maria,
34
Friederich, 34

Philip, 34
GERGERICH,
Annamaria, 25
Catharine, 23, 25
John, 25
Margaret, 23
Philip, 23
GERMANNE, Anna
Margaretha, 70
Catharina Elisabeta
70
Joseph, 70
Juliana, 70
GERTIG, Georg, 83
Magdalen, 83
Michael, 83
GILCHRIST,
Eleanor, 61
Jean, 58
John, 59
Martha, 58
Matthew, 59
GILLMOR, Moses,
59
GINDER,
Elisabetha, 56
GLEN, Elizabeth, 62
GLONINGER,
Catherine, 11
Philip, 11
GOELLER,
Margaret, 52
Margaretha
Dorothea 52
Michael, 52
GOETZ, Joannes, 72
GOMSERT, John, 18
GOORLY, John, 59
GORLITZ, Anna
Maria Magdalena

HAAG, Barbara, 49
Cath., 87
Catharina, 89
Georg Michael, 45
Joh. Georg, 89
Joh. Philip, 89
Johanne, 87
Johannes, 45
Juliana, 87
Mathias, 49
Mattheus, 87
Philip, 87
Susanna, 49, 87
HAAK, Anna Maria,
82
Barb. Deibler(in),
85
Catharina, 81, 82
G. Mich., 82
Juliana Popp(in),
84
Magd., 28, 82
Maria Sussanna, 85
Matheis, 85
Mattheus, 85
Michael, 81
Michel, 81
Philipp, 84, 85
Sussanna, 85
HAAS, Catherine, 5
John, 5
William, 5
HABERLING,
Catharina, 35
Friederich, 35
HACK, Go., 29
HACKER, Adam, 3,
8
Anna Barbara, 3
Anna Maria, 8

Catherine, 6
George, 8
John, 6
Maria, 3
Martin, 79
Sarah, 6
HACKERT, Frid., 81
HAEN, Johannes, 48
Margaretha, 48
Sarah, 48
HAENNING,
George, 6
Jacob, 6
Magdalene, 6
HAG, Catharina, 44
Daniel, 44
Georg Michael, 44
Mathais, 44
Peter, 44
Susanna, 44
HAHN, Adam, 24,
25
Anna Maria, 15, 45
Cath., 31
Christ., 31
Christian, 35
Christina, 15, 35
Christine, 32
Elisabeth, 35
Eva, 24
Eva Elizabeth, 25
Heinrich, 15
Henrich, 44
Jacob, 31, 32, 35
Johannes, 35
Magd. Catharina,
31
Mar. Sarah, 86
Maria Eliz., 2
Sarah, 24, 44

Susanna, 30
HAIER, Catherine,
1, 3
George, 1, 3
Susanna, 3
HAIN, Catharine, 20
George, 20
HAMAN,
Margaretha, 88
Philip, 88
HAMILTON, Hugh,
59
Thomas, 59
William, 59
HAMMACHER,
Adam, 30, 32, 33
Cath., 30, 32
Jacob, 30
M. Cath., 33
M. Catharina, 32
Maria Magdalena,
33
HAMMAN, Johan
Philip, 48
Maria Margretha,
48
HANN, Catharina,
50
Elisabetha, 50
Greth, 50
Johannes, 43, 47,
50
Margareth, 43
Margreth, 47
Sarah, 47, 50
HARMAN, Barbara,
16
Catharina, 65
HARRIS, Elizabeth,
59

Andreas, 31
Elisabeth, 29
George, 29
Johannes, 31
Rosina, 29
HEINECKE, Casper,
19
Magdalena, 19
HEISS, Barbara, 4,
6
Jacob, 13
John, 4, 6
Magdalene, 13
Susanna, 4
HEIST, Barbara, 8
John, 8
HELD, Georg, 40
Joh. Georg, 40
Magdalena, 40
HELLER, Adam, 85
Anna Maria, 50
Catharina, 47, 80,
81, 84, 86
Isaac, 47, 80, 81,
84, 86
Maria, 84
Susanna, 89
HEMBERLE, Anton,
70
HEN, Peter, 45
HENDEL, Rev., 53
HENDERSON,
James, 60
HENN, Henrich, 43
Jacob, 43
Maria, 43
HENNEY, John
Michael, 53
HENNING, Jacob,
12

Magdalene, 12
Margaret, 12
HENNSON,
Catharine, 23
William, 23
HERAUF, Andreas,
75
Eliesabeta, 75
Sallme, 75
HERAUFF, Andreas,
40
Antony, 40
Maria Elizabetha,
40
HERMAN, Anna, 42
Anna Margareta,
41
Anna Margaretha,
42
Catharina, 44, 49
Dav., 83
David, 84
Elisabeth, 49, 83,
84
Elisabetha, 49
Georg, 44, 46
Jac., 84
Jacob, 41, 42
Jakob, 88
Johannes, 42, 49
John, 44
Jonas, 84
Marg., 84
Margaretha, 41, 88
Margreth, 84
Susanna, 49
HERMANN, A.
Catharina, 88
Catharina, 81, 88
David, 53, 80, 81

Elisabeth, 53, 81
Georg, 87
Jacob, 53
Jakob, 88
Johann Daniel, 80
Joseph, 53
Magdalena, 88
Margaretha, 53
Rahel, 88
HERRMAN, A.
Maria, 47
Catharina, 43
Jacob, 41, 47
Joh. Adam, 87
Johann Philip, 41
Johannes, 47, 87
Margareta, 41
Margretha, 47
HERTER, Anna
Maria, 53
Matthais, 30
HERTZ, Ludwig, 14
Maria Rosina, 14
HETERICH, Adam,
30
M. Margd., 30
HETHERICK,
Adam, 27
Joh. Nicholaus, 27
Mary, 27
HETHERINGTON,
Alexander 60
HETTERICH, Adam,
32, 36
Eva Elisabeth, 32
Hanna, 32
Leonard, 36
M. Marg., 36
Marg., 32
Peter, 32

JOHNSTON, Jane,
61
JONSLY, Anna
Maria, 10
Susanna, 10
Walter, 10
JORAI, Salome, 56
JORAY, Abraham,
53
Hannah, 53
Samuel (F.), 53
JORIA, Abraham, 57
JUND, An. Maria,
34
Anna Maria, 36
Barbara, 34
Daniel, 34, 36
Dorath, 33
Nicholaus, 33
Salome, 33
JUNG, An. Maria,
33
Christian, 5
Elisabetha, 44
Wilhelm, 44

-K-
KAHN, Margaretha,
56
Maria, 56
KALEY, Christian,
77
Johannes, 77
Wilhelm Morrison,
77
KALNAT, Elizabeth,
21
Thomas, 21
KAMERER,
Christian, 78, 79

Susanna, 78
KAMMERER,
Catarina, 78
Dietrich, 78
KAMP, David, 78
Jacob, 78
KAPP, John, 10
Samuel, 10
Sarah, 10
KARMENIE, Joseph,
74
KAUB, Elizabeth, 10
Peter, 10
KEARSLEY, Peggy,
58
Samuel, 60
KEHSINGER,
Michael, 70
KEISEN, Elisabeth,
27
KEISS, A. Maria, 28
Catharine, 28
Elisabeth, 28
Hannes, 33
Henrich, 28
Johannes, 29
KELKER, Frederick,
13
Lydia, 13
KELLER, Antoni, 38
Barbara, 38
Elizabeth, 3, 8, 11,
17
Joseph, 3, 8, 17
KELSO, John, 60
William, 60
KENNEDY, David,
60
Sarah, 59
KEPLINGER,

Barbara, 20
Jacob, 20, 21
Maria Barbara, 20
KEPLINGR,
Barbara, 21
KERBERIN,
Elisabetha, 79
KERMANNE,
Antoni, 71
Antonj, 71
Joann Martin, 71
Joann Philipp, 71
Joannes, 71
KERN, Catharine,
21
Elizabeth, 18
Jacob, 21
Sophia, 18
Thomas, 18, 21
KESSINGERIN,
Anna Maria 72
KETCH, James, 38
Sussannah, 38
KETERRING, Jacob,
67
Margareth, 67
KETTENRING,
Jacob, 67
Joann Eberhard, 74
KETTERING, Jacob,
40, 74
Joann Adam, 69
KEYS, Robert, 60
KIBLINGER,
Abalona, 23
Bar., 25
Elizabeth, 2, 12, 25
Henrich, 23
Jacob, 25
Johannes, 25

LANNING, John, 60
LARUE, Barbara, 38
  Barbarah, 38
LASCH, Adam, 42
  Andr., 30
  Elisabetha, 42
  Ma. Magdalena, 30
  Magd., 30
  Magdalena, 33
  Maria Catharina,
  33
  Stephan, 33
  Susanna, 42
LAUBER, Baltaser,
  37
  Balthaser, 39
  Balthazer, 40
  Elizabeth, 37, 39,
  40
  Johan Adam, 37
  Johan Frederick,
  39
  Johanes, 37
  Johann Heinrich,
  40
LAUDERMILCH,
  Adam, 65
  Catharina, 65
  Johannes, 65
LAUTENSCHLAGE
  R, Jacob, 46
  Sophia, 46
LE CRONE,
  Philippina
  Margaretha, 56
LE RUH, Jonas, 69
  Margareta, 69
LEBKUCHLER,
  Catarina, 77
  David, 77

Henrich, 76
Johanne, 77
Joseph, 77
Michel, 76, 77
Susanna, 76, 77
LEFFLER, Cath., 31
  Philip, 31
LEICHT, Catharina,
  55
LEIM, Catharine, 18
  Michael, 18
LEIM , Catharine
  Elisabetha 15
  Elisabeth, 15
  Micheal, 15
LEINBACH,
  Christine, 14
  John, 4
  Maria, 4
LENCKER, A.
  Maria, 82, 84
  Adam, 82, 84, 85
  An. Maria, 84, 85
  Elisabeth, 84, 85
  J. Adam, 82
  Jacob, 85
  Johann Michael, 84
  Johann Philipp, 85
  Johannes, 82
  Magdalena, 85
  Phil., 84
  Philipp, 85
  Stephan, 85
  Sussanna, 85
LENGEL, Catherine,
  1
  Elizabeth, 1
  Martin, 1
LENHART, Peter,
  23

LENKERT, A. Cath.,
  89
  A. Maria, 89
  A. Rosina, 89
  Adam, 89
  Elisabeth, 89
  Jakob, 89
LENNERT,
  Elizabeth, 18
  Frederick, 18
  Maria, 18
LENTZ, A. Maria, 26
  Anna Maria, 67
  Jacob, 66, 67
LENZ, Jacob, 67, 69
LEOBOLT,
  Friedrich, 45
LEPPO, Catharina,
  89
  Peter, 89
LERCH, Anna
  Margaretha, 51
  Catherine, 23
  Christoph, 51
  John, 23
LERG (BERG),
  Anna Catharina,
  85
  Elisabeth, 85
  Geor., 85
  Georg, 85
  Peter, 85
LERKIN, John, 60
LERRUH, Anna
  Maria, 2
  George, 2
LERU, George, 6
  John George, 1
  Maria, 1, 6
LERUH, Anna

MCCLEASTER,
James, 60
MCCLURE, Andrew,
60
Elizabeth, 59
Francis, 60
Joseph, 60
Richard, 60
MCCORD, Flora, 61
Samuel, 61
MCCORMICK,
James, 61
Martha, 61
William, 61
MCCRUNY, Anna
Magdalena, 48
Johannes, 48
Jonathan, 48
Maria, 48
Maria Catharina, 48
Maria Elizabetha,
48
Polly, 48
Sarah, 48
Samuel, 48
MCCULLOM,
Alexander, 61
MCDONALD, John,
61
MCELHENNY,
William, 61
MCELVAIN,
Elizabeth, 13
John, 13
MCFADDEN, James,
61
MCFARLAND,
Elizabeth, 62
Mary, 60
MCGAHON, John,

40
Mary, 40
Thomas, 40
MCGUIRE, Richard,
61
MCHADDEN,
William, 61
MCHARGUE,
Margaret, 61
MCKALLENS,
Joannes, 72
M'KENNY, Barbara,
86
John, 86
Mary, 86
MCKINNEY,
Charles, 78
Nancy, 59
Patrick, 78
MCKINZIE, James,
61
MACLAY, Samuel,
60
William, 60
MCLEIN, James, 42
Magdalena, 42
MCLEN, Catharina,
55
MCLIEN, Catharina,
41
Jonas, 41
Magdalena, 41
MCNAIR, Thomas,
61
MCNAMARA,
James, 61
MCNEAL, Elizabeth,
61
MCQUOWN
(MCEWEN), John

61
MCTEER, Samuel,
61
MAJER, Adam, 72
Catarina, 71
Hennrich, 71
Magdalena, 71
MANZ, Stolfel, 68
MARTER,
Elisabetha, 46
Joh. Philip, 46
Johannes, 46, 88
Salome, 88
MARTIN, Anna
Sabina, 1
Elisabeth, 54
Johannes, 54
John, 18
John Nicholas, 1
Maria Regina, 1
Michel, 43
Regina, 1, 18
MARTN, Patty, 12
MARTTER, A.
Catharina, 89
A. Maria, 89
Catharina, 89
Daniel, 89
Elisabeth, 89
Georg, 89
Jakob, 89
Joh., 89
Michael, 89
MARTY, Elisabeth,
34
Joh., 34
Johann Martin, 34
MASS, Cathrina, 37
Johan Peter, 37
Johan Philip, 37

John Henry, 19
Julia, 19
Julia Ann, 19
Juliann, 17
Magdalene, 2
Maria Barbara, 19
Maria Elizabetha,
  38
Michael, 26
MEYERS, Barara, 18
  Catharine
  Elizabeth 19
  Henry, 19
  Jacob, 18
  Julia Ann, 19
MEZGAR, Anna
  Maria, 38
  John, 38
MICHAEL,
  Catharine, 25
  Elizabeth, 25
  John, 25
  Sarah, 25
MICHEL, Etwina, 23
  Jacob, 23
MIESCH, Catherine,
  6
  John, 6, 8, 10
  Magdalene, 6, 8, 10
MILLER, Anna, 82
  Anna Maria, 42, 43,
  82
  Catharina, 42
  Christdinna, 75
  Christina, 43
  Daniel, 43
  Elisabeth, 64, 65
  Elisabetha, 49
  Elizabeth, 2, 11
  Heinrich, 40

Jacob, 14, 47, 49,
  75
Johannes, 47, 75
John, 18, 64
Jonathan, 42, 43,
  82
Joseph, 65
Jost, 65
Magdalena, 40
Margaret, 18
Peter, 2
Sarah, 47, 49
Sussana, 82
Thomas, 61
MILLISEN, Jacob,
  21
  Maria, 21
MINCH, Anna
  Barbara, 46
  Anna Maria, 46
  Georg, 46
MING, Maria, 12
MISCH, Margaret, 4
MITCHEL, David,
  61
MITSCHEL,
  Christian, 75, 76
MOHR, Barbara, 17
  Thomas, 17
MONTGOMERY,
  James, 61
MONTIETH, James,
  61
MOODY, Robert, 61
MOOR, Johannes,
  40, 89
  Margretha, 40
  Patrick, 40
  Philippina, 89
MOORE, Anna, 62

Barbara, 17, 18
Frances, 62
Fronica, 76
John, 17, 18
John Peter, 17
John Thomas, 17
Thomas, 76
William, 61
MORDAH, Eleanor,
  58
MORELL, Dieterich,
  72
  Fridrich, 70
  J. Dietrich, 66
MORREL, Jo
  Dietrich, 71
MORRISON, John,
  61
MORTON, Sally, 60
MORVY, Bernard, 3
  Jacoby, 3
MULLER, A. Maria,
  88
  Anna, 88
  Anna Maria, 48
  Johannes, 88
  Jonathan, 48, 88
  Magdalena, 48
MUNG, Barbara, 41
  Catharina
  Elisabetha 41
  Georg, 41
MUNICH, Georg, 51
  Maria Barbara, 51
  Maria Margaretha,
  51
MUNIG, Anna, 54
  Georg, 54
MURRAY, Margaret,
  62

An. Maria, 83, 86
Anna Catharina, 82
Anna catharine, 65
Anna Maria, 46, 83
Barbara, 56
Catharina, 41, 54,
82, 83, 84, 85
David, 83
Elisabeth, 81, 88
Fridrich, 82
Fried., 80
Friedrich, 41
Georg, 82, 83, 84,
85, 87
George, 54
Heinrich, 65
Isaac, 84
J. Georg, 87
Johann Jacob, 83
Johannes, 65, 82
Jonas, 85
Joseph, 46, 81, 83,
86
Margareth, 65
Maria, 81, 88
Maria Magdalena,
86
Maria Margareth,
80
Martin, 88
Salome, 80, 82, 88
Sophia, 88
PEEHSS, Cath., 33
Eva Elisabeth, 33
Hen., 33
PEFFER, Catherine,
8
George, 8, 14
Samuel, 14
Susanna, 14

Susanna Maria, 8
PEIFFER, Philip, 13
PETER, Clara, 43,
45
Elisab., 84
Elizabeth, 3
Hannes, 23
Michael, 3
Rudolf, 43
Rudolph, 45
PETRI, Sorer, 38
PETRY, Catherine, 8
Henry, 8, 11
John, 11
Magdalene, 8, 11
PFANENKUCHEN,
Cathrina, 40
Rosina Cathrina, 40
PFANNENKUCHE
N, Joann Peter, 73
PFEILIN, Catarina,
79
PFLICHT, Christine,
6
Frederick, 6
PFRENNER,
Elizabeth, 25
John George, 25
Susanna Christiana
25
PFRIMMER, John
George, 4
Samuel, 4
PFUHL, John, 5
John Jacob, 5
Mary Magdalene, 5
PHEES, Cath., 36
PHILLIPI,
Catharine, 18
Elisabeth, 18

Michael, 18
PINKERTON,
David, 61
Mary, 58
PITTERMANN, A.
Margareth, 84
Baltz., 81, 84
Margareth, 81
PLAUCK, Eva, 24
PLUMKET,
Elizabeth, 60
PLUNKET, William,
61
POHL, Anna
Barbara Elizabeth,
18
Fanny, 18
Henry, 18
Margaret, 18
POLING, Fanny, 18
POLK, James Smith,
61
POOL, John, 6
Polly, 6
Samuel, 6
POOP (BOBB),
Elizabeth, 20
Eva Catharine, 20
Peter, 20
POORMAN, Anna
Maria, 19
Christiana, 20
Christina, 21
Daniel, 20, 21
Elizabeth, 19
Jacob, 21
Maria, 19
Maria Elizabeth, 20
Michael, 19
Polly, 20

Michael, 46, 47
SALATIN, Christina,
44
Michael, 44
SALENTIN,
Catharina, 85
Johannes, 85
SALIDE, Christina,
51
Michael, 51
SALLADE,
Christina, 43, 44
Jacob, 46
Joh., 35
Margaretha, 35
Michael, 43, 44
Susanna, 46
SALLADEE, Daniel,
43
Margreth, 43
Maria, 43
SALLATE,
Johannes, 42
Margretha, 42
Simon, 42
SALLEDY, Michael,
52
SALLENTIN, Christ.
Doroth., 82
Christ. Dorthea, 83
Christina, 81
Johs, 81
Mich., 81, 82, 83
SAMBRE, Barbara,
86
C. Magdalena, 86
Eva Maria, 86
Johannes, 86
SAWYER, Joseph,
62

Mary, 62
William, 62
SCARLET,
Catherine, 14
Henry, 14
SCHAAFSTALL,
Catharina, 45
Peter, 45
Susanna, 45
SCHACKY, Anna
Barbara, 3
George, 3
SCHAD, And., 35
Elisabeth, 35
SCHADEL, Anna
Magdalena, 80
Johann Henrich, 81
Johannes, 48
Maria, 80, 81
Mich., 81
Michael, 48
Michel, 80
SCHAEFER, Frena
(Verena), 10
George, 65
Maria, 65
SCHAEFFER,
Margaret, 13
Susanna, 13
William, 8, 13
SCHAETEL,
Charlotte, 56
Michael, 56
SCHAFER, Barbara,
23
Conrad, 23
Daniel, 23
Elisabeth, 30
Georg, 64
Jacob, 85

Johannes, 78
Margreth, 85
Maria, 64
Michael, 78
SCHAFFER, Anna
Ferena, 38
Christina Barbara,
40
Elisabeth, 65
Georg, 65
Georg Michael, 40
Heinrich, 38
Henry, 38
Maria, 65
Michael, 40
SCHAFFSTALL,
Catharina, 45
Peter, 45
SCHAFSTAL, Peter,
50
SCHAFSTALL,
Cath., 47
Catharina, 47, 49
Elisabeth, 46, 88
Elisabetha, 44
Henrich, 44, 46, 88
Johannes, 46
Magdalena, 47
Peter, 47, 49
Regina, 88
Sarah, 44
Simon, 49
SCHAHBERGER,
Jacob, 6
Nicholas, 6
SCHALLHAMER,
George, 2
Magdalene, 2
SCHALLIN,
Catharina Marg.,

An. Maria, 30, 81
Anna Maria, 17, 20, 34, 53
Barbara, 20
Cath., 18
Catharina, 36
Catharine, 23
Christiana, 18, 24
Christina, 34, 36
Christine, 23
Conrad, 23
Elisabeth, 34
Elizabeth, 18
Eva, 25
Eve, 19
George, 19
Hanna, 81
Henry, 20
Jacob, 28, 81
Johannes, 30
John, 18
John George, 20, 25
John Peter, 25
Justina, 18
Lorenz, 19
Maria, 17
Maria Agnes, 18
Mathias, 20
Michael, 18
Peter, 28, 30, 34, 35, 36, 53
Philip, 17, 18
Susanna, 74
Thomas, 24
SCHMIT, Maria
   Margaret, 5
   Nicholas, 5
SCHMITH,
   Margaret, 11

SCHMITT, Anna, 25
   Anna Maria, 15, 42
   Christina, 25
   Christina Elizabeth 25
   Conrad, 2
   Elisabeth, 25
   Eva, 24
   George, 24
   Hannah, 42
   Heinrich, 15
   John, 2
   Margaret, 2, 9
   Maria Margaret, 9
   Michael, 25
   Peter, 42
   Thomas, 25
SCHNEIDER, A.
   Maria, 28, 30
   Abraham, 28
   Adam, 77
   Agnes, 56
   Anna, 7
   Anna Maria, 49, 53
   Cath., 88
   Catharina, 47, 57, 82, 87, 88
   Catherine, 11
   Daniel, 7
   Elisabeth, 77, 85
   Georg, 87
   Gerthraut, 85
   Gottfried, 47
   Hannah, 57
   J. Georg, 85
   Jacob, 47, 53
   Jakob, 87
   Jo. Nicolaus, 30
   Joann Adam, 68
   Joh. Dieterich, 53

Johan Nicolaus, 30
Johannes, 87
John, 13
John Peter, 7
Leonard, 49
Leonhard, 82
Leonhart, 50
Magdalena, 56
Nicholas, 28
Samuel, 49, 82
Sebastian, 14
Simon, 8, 11
Stophel, 50
SCHNEITER,
   Ludwig, 6
   Rosina, 6
SCHNELL, A.
   Catharine, 26
   Jacob, 26
   Mar Barbara, 26
SCHNOCK,
   Elisabeth, 84
   Marg., 84
   Pet., 84
SCHNUG, Anna
   Christiana, 53
   Catharine, 80
   Christ., 80
   Christian, 47, 53, 80, 84
   Elisabetha, 47
   Johann Adam, 53
   Johannes, 80
   Magdalen, 80
   Margaretha
   Jager(in) 84
   Philippina, 80
SCHOCK, Greta
   (Margareth), 43
   Johann Henrich, 43

Christoph, 74
Daniel, 74
Elisabetha, 74
Elizabeth, 2, 8
Frederick, 8
Georg, 74
George, 8
Jacob, 2
John, 8
John Adam, 8
Lowisa, 74
Maria Barbara, 74
Maria Sara, 74
SCHURA, Samuel, 52
SCHUSSLE,
Catharina, 53
Jacob, 53
SCHUSTER, Anna
Barbara 55
SCHUTZ, Anna
Maria Lentzin 67
Cathrina, 42
Elisabetha, 42
Jacob, 67
Ludwig, 42, 53
Maria Elisabeth, 53
SCHUY, Ann
Catharine, 26
Annamaria, 25
Daniel, 26
Fred, 23
Henrich, 25
Jacob, 26
John, 26
John Jacob, 23
Rebecca, 26
Salome, 26
Veronica, 23
SCHUZ, J. Georg,

66
SCHWAB, A. Maria, 89
Jacob, 89
Wilhelm, 89
SCHWALM,
Andrew, 1
Catharina, 36
Joh., 36
John Philip, 1
Otilia Magd., 36
Susanna, 1
SCHWARTZ,
Abraham, 27
Adam, 27, 29, 31
Casper, 1
Christina, 29
Elizabeth, 1, 27
John, 1
Leonard, 1
Maria, 31
Michael, 27
Rosina, 27, 31
Sara, 27
SCHWEICKARDT,
Andreas 57
SCHWEICKERT,
Catherine, 7, 10
Daniel, 7, 10
George, 7, 10
SCHWEIGART
(SWEIGARD),
Adam, 65
Anna, 65
Anna Barbara, 65
Anna Maria, 65
Daniel, 66
Johann, 66
Johann Georg, 65
Johann Michael, 65

Johann Peter, 65
Johannes, 65
Maria, 65, 66
Peter, 65
SCHWEIGERT,
Adam, 56, 66
Andreas, 65
Maria, 66
Peter, 65
SCHWEITZER,
Catharine, 17, 18
Catherine, 3, 7
Daniel, 3
Elizabeth, 12, 20
Frederick, 3, 17, 18, 20
John Adam, 17
SCHWENCK, Affre, 2
Christian, 2
SCHWEYGER, Anna
Christina, 39
Jonas, 39
Peter, 39
SEIDER, Barbara, 21
SEIDERS, Jacob, 19
SEIFER, Anthony, 12
SEILER, Catherine, 6
Henry, 6
John, 6
SEMER, Maria, 14
SEMPLE, Sarah, 58
SENGER, Chaterina, 75
Chunrath, 75
Chunrod, 75
Conrath, 74

Leonhart, 49
SNIDER, Catharine, 20
George, 20
John, 20
Magdalena, 20
SNODGRASS, John, 62
SNYDER, Anna
  Christiana, 18
  Elisabeth, 18
  John Valentine, 18
SOMMERLAD,
  Anna Elisabeth, 47
  Anna Magdalena, 47
  Valentin, 47
SOMMERLADE, An.
  Elisabeth, 84
  Hanna, 84
  Valantin, 84
SOREMLY
  (WORMELY),
  Anna, 8
  Elizabeth, 8
  George, 8
SPAD, Michael, 77, 78
SPANG, Johan, 76, 79
  Susanna, 76
  Wilhelm, 79
SPAT, Elis., 89
SPATH, Anna
  Elisabeth, 47
  Cathrina, 38
  Christian, 38
  Christina, 38
  Elisabeth, 44
SPEIDEL, Barbara,

68, 75
Catarina Barbara, 73
Christian, 76
Christina, 68
Daniel Speittel, 75
David, 77
Eliesabet, 75
Elisabeth, 73
Elisabetha, 67
Georg, 68
Jacob, 67, 68, 72, 73, 75, 76
Joann Adam, 68
Johan Gorg, 75
Johan Jorg, 67
Johan Peter, 67
Johannes, 67, 68, 77
Machsmilianus, 74
Magdalena, 68, 75
Margaretha, 67, 68
Maria Elisabetha, 68
Max, 68, 76
Maximilian, 67, 69, 73, 76, 77
Maximilianus, 75
Maxmilian, 67, 68
Michael, 79
Sawina, 75
Susanna, 67, 76
Wielhelm, 75
Wilhelm, 77
Willhelm, 75
William, 79
SPEIDELL,
  Elisabetha, 67
  Jacob, 67
SPEITEL,

Margareth, 67
Maxmilian, 67
SPEITELIN,
  Margareth, 67
SPENCE, James, 62
  Jean, 63
SPENGLER,
  Christine, 8, 10
  Eva, 8
  Georg, 67
  Joseph, 10
  Martin, 10
  Martinus, 8
  Peter, 67
SPIEGEL, Maria
  Barbara 54
SPOHN, Catharine, 23, 24
  Catherine, 3
  Gotleib, 24
  Gottlieb, 3, 23
  Jacob, 3
  Sara Susanna, 24
SPRING, Hannah, 79
  Nicklaus, 75
STAAL, Anna Maria, 67
  Elizabeth, 67
  Frid., 67
  Fridrich, 67
  Mar. Elisabeth, 67
  Mattheus, 67
STAALMAN,
  Joseph, 46
  Nellena, 46
  Rebecca, 46
STAENZ, Anna
  Elizabeth, 3
  Elizabeth, 3

Elisabetha, 52
Eva Maria, 54
Jost, 52
Leonhardt, 54
Philip, 55
Susanna, 54
STIEGER, Maria
Marg., 52
STOBERLEIN,
Daniel, 56
Georg, 56
Justus, 56
Leonard, 56
Philippina
Margaretha, 56
STOBERLIN, Anna
Margaretha, 51
Jost, 51
STOEBER, Barbara,
20
Benjamin, 20
Casper, 20
Eve, 20
STOEVER, Casper,
21
Eva, 21
John Casper, 21
STOLL, Margaretha,
69
Matheis, 69
STOVER, Caspar, 23
Eva, 23
Gottlieb, 23
STRASER, Conrad,
7
Esther, 7
Simon, 7
STRICKER,
Cathrina, 40
Jacob, 9, 40

STRICKLER, Jacob,
51
Willm, 70
STRIKER, Barbara,
40
Lorenz, 40
STRIKLER,
Dorothea, 51
Valentin, 51
STROCK, Catharine,
18
Christiana, 18
John, 18
John Conrad, 18
STROH, John, 3
Maria, 3
Nicholas, 3
STROHSCHEIDER,
An. Maria, 30
STROHSCHNEIDE
R, Anna Maria, 32
G. Jacob, 30
Johannes, 30, 32,
34
M. Elisabeth, 30,
32, 34
Magdalena, 34
STROHSCHNITTE
RIN Barbara, 33
STUBERLING,
Daniel, 53
Eva Elisabeth, 53,
54
Eva Maria, 53
Johan Leonhardt,
53, 54
STUCKY, Michael,
76
STUENTZ,
Elizabeth, 2

STUENTZE, Anna
Elizabeth, 2
Henry, 2
STURGEON, Lydia,
61
STUTZMAN,
Christian, 27, 42
Eliszabeth, 42
Elizabeth, 27
Johannes, 42
STUTZMANIN,
Cath., 27
STUTZMENIN,
Elizabeth 31
STUTZMENNIN,
Magd., 36
SWAN, Hugh, 62
William, 62
SWARRTZ, Adam,
27
Isaak, 27
Rosina, 27

-T-
TAGGART, Robert,
62
TEMPLETON,
Hannah, 62
Robert, 62
TEUBLER,
Catharina, 45
Matheis, 45
THOM, Esther, 58
Margaret, 62
THOMPSON,
James, 62
John, 62
Samuel, 62
TICE, John, 18
TIDTRIG, Johan

51
Johan Philip, 51
Magdalena, 51
VOGHT, Eva, 39
Jonas, 39
VOGT, George, 20
Maria, 20
VON KENNEN,
Michael, 2, 3
VOUGHT, Eleanor,
60

-W-
WACHS,
Margaretha, 55
WACKER, Anna, 79
Johannes, 79
Mar. Salome 79
WAGNER, A. Maria,
31
Anna Maria, 19
Barbara, 19
Catharina, 52
Joh. Crist. Fried.
31
John Christian, 19
M. Magdalena, 31
Margaret, 4
Maria Eva, 56
Maria Margaret, 4
Sebastian, 4
WAGONER, Adam,
37
Cath., 36
George, 36
Jacob, 36
Rosina, 37
WAIFIELD,
Barbara, 14
WALBORN, Anna

Maria, 20
Catharine, 23, 24
Catherine, 4, 7
Christian, 20, 21
Elisabeth, 20
Elizabeth, 21, 24
Henrich, 23
Henry, 4, 23
Margaret, 24
Michael, 23, 24
Peter, 4, 7
Sarah, 21
WALER, Adam, 72
WALKER, James, 62
Prudence, 62
WALL, Eliz., 38
Elizabeth, 38
John, 38
Mary, 38
William, 38
Willm., 38
WALLACE, Ann
Maria, 61
Elizabeth, 58
Isabella, 59
James, 62
Moses, 62
William, 62
WALLAUER,
Charlotte, 4
Leonard, 10
Magdalene, 10
Susanna, 10
WALTER, Abraham,
37
Jacob, 4, 37
Juliana, 37
Peter, 4
WARNER, Anna
Maria, 47

Georg, 47
Johannes, 47, 48
Margaretha, 48
Margretha, 47
WATSON, David, 62
WATZ , Christine,
23
Jacob, 23
John, 23
WEBER, An. Maria,
82
Anna Maria, 16, 48,
51, 52, 54
Catharina, 45, 48,
74, 89
Heinrich, 16
Jacob, 51, 52, 54
Joh. Jacob, 45
Johann George, 54
Jon., 82
Magdalena, 16, 50,
52
Margaretha, 51
Maria Magdalena,
85
Martin, 53
Peter, 45, 48, 50,
89
WEEBER, Elisabeta,
72
Georg, 72
Joann Georg, 72
WEIBEL, Anna
Maria, 8
Catherine, 8
George, 8
WEIMAR,
Magdalena, 86
Matthias, 86
WEIMER, Anna, 69

Heritage Books by F. Edward Wright:

Lancaster County, Pennsylvania, Church Records of the 18th Century, Volume 5

Lancaster County, Pennsylvania, Church Records of the 18th Century: Volume 6
Robert L. Hess and F. Edward Wright

*Lancaster County, Virginia, Marriage References
and Family Relationships, 1650–1800*

Land Records of Sussex County, Delaware, 1769–1782

Land Records of Sussex County, Delaware, 1782–1789: Deed Book N No. 13
Elaine Hastings Mason and F. Edward Wright

Marriage Licenses of Washington, District of Columbia, 1811–1830

*Marriage References and Family Relationships of Charles City,
Prince George, and Dinwiddie Counties, Virginia, 1634–1800*

Marriages and Deaths from Eastern Shore Newspapers, 1790–1835

*Marriages and Deaths from the Newspapers of Allegany
and Washington Counties, Maryland, 1820–1830*

Marriages and Deaths from the York Recorder, *1821–1830*

*Marriages and Deaths in the Newspapers of Frederick
and Montgomery Counties, Maryland, 1820–1830*

*Marriages and Deaths in the Newspapers of
Lancaster County, Pennsylvania, 1821–1830*

*Marriages and Deaths in the Newspapers of
Lancaster County, Pennsylvania, 1831–1840*

Marriages and Deaths of Cumberland County, [Pennsylvania], 1821–1830

Marriages, Births, Deaths and Removals of New Castle County, Delaware

Maryland Calendar of Wills:
*Volume 9: 1744–1749; Volume 10: 1748–1753; Volume 11: 1753–1760;
Volume 12: 1759–1764; Volume 13: 1764–1767; Volume 14: 1767–1772;
Volume 15: 1772–1774; and Volume 16: 1774–1777*

*Maryland Eastern Shore Newspaper Abstracts
Volume 1: 1790–1805; Volume 2: 1806–1812;
Volume 3: 1813–1818; Volume 4: 1819–1824;
Volume 5: Northern Counties, 1825–1829*
F. Edward Wright and Irma Harper;
*Volume 6: Southern Counties, 1825–1829;
Volume 7: Northern Counties, 1830–1834*
Irma Harper and F. Edward Wright;
Volume 8: Southern Counties, 1830–1834

*Maryland Eastern Shore Vital Records:
Book 1: 1648–1725, Second Edition; Book 2: 1726–1750; Book 3: 1751–1775;
Book 4: 1776–1800; and Book 5: 1801–1825*

*Maryland Militia in the War of 1812:
Volume 1: Eastern Shore; Volume 2: Baltimore City and County;
Volume 3: Cecil and Harford Counties; Volume 4: Anne Arundel and Calvert Counties;
Volume 5: St. Mary's and Charles Counties; Volume 6: Prince George's County;
and Volume 7: Montgomery County*

Maryland Militia in the Revolutionary War
S. Eugene Clements and F. Edward Wright